T0170907

THE BASIC COOKBOOK

THE BASIC COOK BOOK GUIDE

compiled by
LESLEY PAGETT

NEW HOLLAND

This edition published in 2109 by New Holland Publishers
First published in 2004 as The Basic Cookbook by New Holland Publishers
London • Sydney • Auckland

131–151 Great Titchfield Street, London WIW 5BB, United Kingdom
1/66 Gibbes Street, Chatswood, NSW 2067, Australia
5/39 Woodside Ave, Northcote, Auckland 0627, New Zealand

newhollandpublishers.com

A record of this book is held at the British Library and the National Library
of Australia.

ISBN 9781760790790

Group Managing Director: Fiona Schultz
Publisher: Fiona Schultz
Designer: Andrew Davies
Cover Design: Yolanda La Gorcé
Production Director: James Mills-Hicks
Printer: Toppan Leefung Printing Limited

10 9 8 7 6 5 4 3 2 1

Keep up with New Holland Publishers on Facebook
facebook.com/NewHollandPublishers

CONTENTS

ACKNOWLEDGMENTS

This is dedicated to my parents
RIP Leslie Wiltshire OAM
RIP Vera Wiltshire OAM

After many years of cooking for my children, I was thrilled to be given the opportunity to publish some of the recipes I prepared for them with so much love. Thank you Nathan, Catherine and Adam — you have been rays of sunshine in my life. Now that you have families of your own, I hope these recipes will be enjoyed by your children and friends.

To Robert, my parents, Susan and Greg, David and AnneMaree, and all the fantastic friends with whom we enjoyed Gourmet Club and special dinners for so long — thank you for all your support and encouragement, and for believing in my ability to conquer.

Lesley

INTRODUCTION

In today's busy world, many of us have forgotten what basic, nutritious home cooking used to be – the food that our mothers and grandmothers prepared in the kitchen from scratch, and the recipes they passed down from generation to generation – dishes that were comforting, delicious and full of goodness.

The Basic Cook Book Guide is a collection of those versatile and simple recipes you grew up with, and how to successfully cook them at home. Being practical and accessible, this cookbook also details directions for the novice cook on how to cook rice, scramble eggs, make stock and bake a cake – and features those all-important conversion charts to ensure that you get the recipe right the first time around. It also contains classic recipes that have stood the test of time – pumpkin soup, shepherd's pie, coleslaw and cheesecake, as well as the delicious curries, stir-fries and casseroles that people enjoy eating today.

So whether you are leaving home and want to learn how to cook, or you just want to create those nostalgic dishes from your childhood, we hope that **The Basic Cook Book Guide** will enable you to enjoy good food at home with great results.

SOUPS

CAULIFLOWER SOUP

1 cauliflower, broken into florets
3 large potatoes, peeled and cut into chunks
750 ml (1⅓ pints) chicken stock or water
1 large onion, chopped
2 carrots, chopped
salt and freshly ground black pepper, to taste
1 x 300 g (10 oz) tub of sour cream

Serves 4–6

Cover cauliflower and potato in chicken stock or water in a pot and boil until soft. Mash vegetables with the liquid, making sure you use enough water to have the consistency of thick soup.

Add onion and carrot to soup. Simmer for 10 minutes. Puree the mixture in a blender or use a bar mix until smooth.

Just before serving, season with salt and pepper and stir in the sour cream. Serve hot with crusty French bread.

CHICKEN NOODLE SOUP

900 ml (1²/₃ pints) chicken stock
1 bay leaf
1 onion, halved
250 g (8 oz) skinless chicken breast
60 g (2 oz) vermicelli, broken into smaller pieces
salt and freshly ground black pepper, to taste
1 tablespoon fresh parsley, chopped, to garnish

Serves 4–6

Put chicken stock, bay leaf, onion and chicken breast into a large saucepan over a high heat. Cook until the mixture is boiling, stirring once or twice. Reduce heat to a simmer and cook for 10 minutes or until chicken is tender.

Lift chicken out of the saucepan with a draining spoon and cut into very small pieces. Lift out onion and bay leaf and discard. Bring stock back to the boil, add vermicelli and cook for 7 minutes or until al dente. Return chopped chicken to the pan and season with salt and pepper, then heat through.

Ladle into warm soup bowls and sprinkle with chopped parsley to serve.

CORN AND CRAB BISQUE

30 g (1 oz) butter
1 teaspoon curry powder
1 x 485 g (15½ oz) can cream of chicken soup
500 ml (1 pint) milk
1 x 250 g (8 oz) can creamy sweet corn
1 x 205 g (6½ oz) can crabmeat, shredded
salt and black pepper, to taste
1 chilli, sliced (optional)
crusty French bread, for serving

Serves 6

In a large saucepan, melt butter, add curry powder and fry over
a low heat for 1–2 minutes. Add chicken soup and milk, stirring
continuously until well blended.

Add sweet corn and bring to the boil. Add shredded crabmeat
and season with salt and pepper. Stir in the sliced chilli, if using.

Serve hot with crusty bread.

CREAMY CHICKEN AND VEGETABLE SOUP

1 roast chicken carcass
900 ml (2 pints) water
1 bay leaf
1 chicken stock cube
salt and freshly ground black pepper, to taste
4 tablespoons fresh cream
2 tablespoons plain (all-purpose) flour
125 g (4 oz) mixed vegetables, cooked and chopped
    (if you have leftover vegetables from a roast,
    these would be perfect)

Serves 4–6

Break chicken carcass into pieces and place in a large saucepan.
Cover with water, add bay leaf, stock cube and salt and pepper.
Bring to the boil over a high heat, then turn down heat to a simmer.
Add cream and flour, stir through, cover with a lid and cook for
1 hour.

Drain contents of saucepan through a colander into a large bowl,
then return liquid to the pan. Discard chicken carcass and bay leaf.
Add cooked vegetables to the liquid. Cook gently for 5 minutes.

SEAFOOD DUMPLING SOUP

1 tablespoon olive oil
2 onions, finely chopped
750 g (1.6 lb) minced gemfish
1 tablespoon anchovy sauce
1 egg, lightly beaten
½ teaspoon salt
½ teaspoon freshly ground
black pepper
2 L (3½ pints) fish stock
2 green onion tops, chopped

Serves 8

Heat the oil in a frying pan, add the onion and cook for 5 minutes.
Place fish into a mixing bowl and add the onion, anchovy sauce,
egg, salt and pepper. Mix well, mold into balls and set to one side.

Bring the fish stock to the boil and then simmer. Add the molded
fish balls to this stock. Simmer for 20 minutes.

Serve in a tureen, or in individual bowls, sprinkled with the
green onion tops.

ICED TOMATO SOUP

3 slices bread, crusts removed
1 kg (2 lb) tomatoes, peeled, deseeded and chopped
1 cucumber, peeled, deseeded and chopped
½ onion, chopped
2 cloves garlic, crushed
½ green capsicum (bell pepper), deseeded and chopped
1 teaspoon salt
1 teaspoon ground cumin
2 tablespoons olive oil
2 tablespoons wine vinegar
GARNISH
1 red or green capsicum (bell pepper), diced
1 small cucumber, diced
1 onion, finely chopped
2 hard-boiled eggs, chopped
croûtons

Serves 6–8

Place all ingredients in a large bowl and allow to stand for
30 minutes to soften bread and blend flavors.

Purée one-third of the mixture at a time in an electric blender
or food processor. Pour back into a bowl and thin down to desired
consistency with 2–3 cups iced water.

Cover and chill well. Adjust seasoning to taste. Serve in chilled
bowls or in a large bowl over ice.

Place garnish ingredients in separate bowls and allow each
diner to add garnish to their own soup.

CREAM OF CHICKEN SOUP

60 g (2 oz) butter
4 tablespoons plain (all-purpose) flour
1.25 L (2 ½ pints) chicken stock
625 ml (21 fl oz) scalded milk (or ½ milk and ½ cream)
1 chicken breast, shredded
1 small stalk celery, finely chopped
few drops Tabasco sauce
salt and freshly ground black pepper, to taste
2 egg yolks
fresh chives, chopped, to serve

Serves 4

Melt butter in a large saucepan, stir in flour and cook for
about 1 minute, then add 625 ml (1 pint) of chicken stock.
Stir continuously over medium heat until boiling. Add remaining
stock, milk, chicken, celery, Tabasco sauce and salt and pepper and
bring to the boil. Reduce heat and simmer, covered, for 5 minutes.

In a bowl, beat egg yolks well with a fork, then pour into a
heated tureen. Pour soup very slowly over egg yolks, stirring all the
time with a wooden spoon.

Sprinkle with some fresh chives. Serve immediately.

CREAM OF MUSHROOM SOUP

250 g (8 oz) mushrooms
125 g (4 oz) butter
½ teaspoon salt
freshly ground black pepper, to taste
3 cloves garlic, finely chopped
1.25 L (2½ pints) chicken stock
150 ml (5 fl oz) fresh cream, at room temperature
garlic-infused croûtons, for serving (see page 27)
parsley, chopped

Serves 4

Before cooking mushrooms, select some of the smallest ones and take a slice from the centre of each so that you have the outline of the mushroom. Put aside to garnish.

Wash mushrooms (do not peel them) and thinly slice. In a frying pan, heat butter to sizzling, then fry mushrooms with salt and a good grind of fresh pepper. Cool, then purée in a blender or food processor with garlic and 250 ml (1 cup) stock.

Pour remaining stock into a large saucepan. Add purée and heat soup to simmering point. Stir in cream. Add reserved mushroom slices and simmer soup for 5 minutes. Taste and adjust seasoning if necessary.

Serve hot with garlic-infused croûtons and a sprinkle of parsley.

FRENCH ONION SOUP

2 kg (4½ lb) lean beef, diced
3.8 L (8 pints) cold water
2 brown onions, sliced
½ bunch celery, coarsely chopped
salt and freshly ground black pepper, to taste
125 g (4 oz) butter
750 g (1½ lb) white onions, thinly sliced
toast, any bread available
375 g (12 oz) cheddar cheese, freshly grated
parsley, finely chopped, to garnish

Serves 8

First make beef stock. Place beef in a large saucepan with water. Bring to the boil, then reduce heat, cover saucepan, and simmer for 1 hour.

Cool stock, then put it into the refrigerator until fat sets on top. Remove surface fat and strain. Return stock to saucepan, add brown onions, celery and salt and pepper, and simmer for a further 3 hours. Strain stock, discarding vegetables, and return to a clean pan.

Preheat oven to 180°C (350°F). Melt butter in a saucepan, add white onion, cover and sauté over a low heat until onion is soft and golden. Stir occasionally with a wooden spoon to prevent catching – there must be no hint of burning. Add sautéed onion to stock and simmer for 1 hour.

Cover base of a large baking or casserole dish or with the thinnest possible slices of toast. Sprinkle the cheese over the toast. Place in the oven for 10 minutes, or until cheese turns into a deep golden crust.

Pour soup into bowls placing a slice of toast carefully on top. Sprinkle with parsley and serve.

GAZPACHO

SOUP
1 large tomato, skinned
1 small cucumber, peeled
1 medium-sized green
   capsicum (bell pepper)
125 ml (4 fl oz) olive oil
60 ml (2 fl oz)
   white vinegar
salt and freshly ground
   black pepper, to taste
3 shallots, thinly sliced
1.85 L (4 pints) beef stock
   (see page 376)

GARLIC-INFUSED
CROÛTONS
4 slices white bread
vegetable oil, for frying
2 cloves garlic, crushed
salt

Serves 6

To make soup, remove seeds from tomato and cucumber, and cut into 1 cm (½ in) pieces. Remove seeds and pith from green capsicum and cut into 1 cm (½ in) pieces.

In a bowl combine oil, vinegar and salt and pepper to taste. Add tomatoes, cucumber, capsicum and sliced shallots. Allow to stand for 1 hour, stirring occasionally so that vegetables absorb dressing.

To make garlic-infused croûtons, remove crusts from bread and cut bread into 1 cm (½ in) cubes. Fry cubes in hot oil with garlic until golden. Drain well, and sprinkle with salt before serving.

Strain vegetables well, then add to beef stock, in a large bowl. Chill thoroughly, then serve with garlic-infused croûtons.

LEEK, POTATO AND BACON SOUP

2.5 kg (5½ lb) potatoes, peeled and cut into chunks
2 leeks, sliced into 3 cm (1 in) rings
½ kg (1 lb) bacon, chopped
salt and freshly ground black pepper, to taste
1 x 300 g (10 fl oz) sour cream
¼ bunch shallots (scallions), chopped
½ bunch coriander (cilantro), chopped

Serves 4–6

Place potatoes in a large saucepan with enough water to cover.
Bring water to the boil and cook potatoes for about 10 minutes
or until soft. Drain water and save. Mash potatoes with the saved
water (adding more water if necessary). The mixture should
have the consist-ency of thick soup. Add leek and bacon to the
mashed potatoes and simmer until leek is soft and bacon is cooked.
Season with salt and pepper.

In a bowl, mix sour cream and shallots. Serve hot, garnished
with coriander.

Variations:

Add your favorite crispy vegetable a few minutes before serving,
add some cream/sour cream to the main body of the soup, or
crisply fry the bacon and add it just before serving.

MINESTRONE

1 kg (2 lb) shin of beef on
  the bone
5 L (10½ pints) water
1 large brown onion,
  sliced
12 black peppercorns
90 g (3 oz) red kidney
  beans (can use tinned)
2 teaspoons salt
1 tablespoon olive oil
2 large tomatoes, skinned
  and quartered
1 stalk celery, sliced
1 carrot, sliced
2 zucchini (courgettes),
  sliced
1 clove garlic, crushed
125 g (4 oz) bacon, diced
1 tablespoon tomato paste
salt and pepper, to taste
60 g (2 oz) spaghetti
  or macaroni
Parmesan cheese,
  for serving

Serves 8

Place beef in a large saucepan with water. Simmer, covered,
for 2 hours with onion, peppercorns, kidney beans and salt.
Skim surface occasionally to clear soup. Meat should be
easily removed from bone when cooking is complete. Cool.
Remove surface fat and onion. Discard bones and return meat
to stock.

Heat oil in a frying pan and sauté tomatoes, celery, carrot and
garlic over a medium heat for 10 minutes. (You may have to add a
little more oil.) Transfer vegetables to stock, and add bacon, tomato
paste and vegetables. Season with salt and pepper and simmer for
40 minutes.

Add spaghetti 8 minutes before cooking is completed.
Sprinkle each serving with grated Parmesan cheese and serve.

PEA AND HAM SOUP

500 g (1 lb) dried split peas
1 kg (2 lb) bacon bones
2.5 L (4½ pints) chicken stock
2 frankfurters
2 teaspoons white vinegar
sliced sour gherkins, to garnish

Serves 8

Soak peas overnight. Drain. Add peas and bacon bones to stock, bring to the boil and simmer for 2½ hours. Cool soup and remove bacon bones. Scrape meat off bones and return meat to soup.

Cook frankfurters in boiling water for 3 minutes. Cool frankfurters, then peel them and cut them into 5 mm (¼ in) slices. Add to soup, with white vinegar. Reheat soup and serve with sour gherkins.

PUMPKIN SOUP

60 g (2 oz) butter
1 white onion, finely chopped
625 ml (2¼ cups) chicken stock
500 g (1 lb) pumpkin, peeled, seeded
    and cut into 5 mm (¼ in) chunks
625 ml (1 pint) hot milk
pinch of ground allspice
salt and freshly ground black pepper, to taste
125 ml (4 fl oz) thickened cream
finely chopped parsley and croûtons to garnish

Serves 8

Melt butter in a large saucepan and gently fry onion for 10 minutes,
or until onion is soft. Add chicken stock and bring to the boil.
Add pumpkin to stock and simmer until tender, about 30 minutes.
Cool. Purée pumpkin in a food processor or blender. Return soup
to pan, add hot milk, allspice, salt and pepper, and heat gently.
Add thickened cream just before serving.

Serve in a tureen, lightly sprinkled with parsley and croûtons.

TOMATO SOUP

2 rashers bacon, chopped
30 g (1 oz) butter (optional)
2 kg (4 lb) ripe tomatoes, skinned and chopped
1 onion, chopped
1 carrot, peeled and grated
1 stick celery, chopped
940 ml (1$\frac{2}{3}$ pints) chicken stock
salt and black pepper, to taste
bouquet garni

Serves 4

Heat bacon in a pan, add butter and melt (if using), then toss
in vegetables and cook. Do not allow bacon or onion to brown.
Add stock, salt and pepper and bouquet garni, then cover soup and
simmer gently for about 35 minutes. Adjust seasoning. Sieve and
reheat, then serve.

SALADS

Salads need not have a special season – simple, easy-to-prepare green salads with a special dressing or mixed vegetable salads make wonderful accompaniments to meats, chicken, fish, omelets, and quiches at any time of the year.

Shredded, or shaped into cups for individual portions, salads also play an important supporting role in the presentation of cold dishes made with other vegetables, meat, poultry, or fish.

The secret to a successful salad is simple: always choose fresh, unblemished ingredients, then prepare them in an imaginative way. Combine flavors and textures carefully and always complement your salads with a compatible dressing.

We know you will enjoy the salads presented in this book. You will find that the recipes contain a variety of ingredients but are simple to prepare. Fine food comes in many guises, but seldom is it as convenient, flavorful, or healthy as when it is gathered from the garden or purchased from a greengrocer with garden-fresh produce.

Fresh fruits and vegetables are relatively inexpensive, easy to prepare, and full of fiber and nutrients. They come in a glorious array of colors, offer a wide range of tastes and textures, and provide raw energy on a sustained level – unlike the quick gratification offered by sugary snacks.

Small wonder that salads – whether simple or carefully composed – are becoming more and more a staple of our daily diet. It is so easy to introduce raw foods in the form of a salad, either at the start of meal, as an accompaniment or, in the French fashion, as a separate course served after the entrée and before the dessert (to cleanse the palate and, equally importantly, to avoid any conflict between the dressing and the wine).

A hearty main-course salad can be a meal in itself, in any season. If you've never sampled a warm salad, now is the time to experience the contrast in textures and temperatures offered by the Lamb and Sesame Seed Salad. And, while fruit salads are conventionally served as desserts, recipes like Avocado and Orange Salad also make excellent savory dishes.

GARLIC SHRIMP SALAD

1 tablespoon extra-virgin olive oil
4 cloves garlic, crushed
½ teaspoon red pepper flakes
24 large shrimp, peeled and deveined
1 medium tomato, sliced
1 head of cos (romaine) lettuce, outer leaves discarded
1 English cucumber, sliced into ribbons
salt and freshly ground black pepper
juice of 1 lime
juice of 1 lemon

Serves 4

Heat a large heavy-based skillet, add the oil, garlic, red pepper flakes and shrimp. Cook, stirring constantly, until the shrimp are cooked, about 3 minutes.

Divide the tomato slices between 4 serving plates, top with lettuces leaves and cucumber ribbons. Add the shrimp and pour over the pan juices. Season with salt and pepper, then squeeze the lemon and lime juices over and serve.

BABY OCTOPUS SALAD

12 baby octopuses
2 teaspoons coriander seeds, toasted
2 cloves garlic, finely minced, plus 12 cloves, sliced
2 tablespoons lemon juice
¼ cup sweet chilli sauce
2 cucumbers, peeled
1 large red capsicum (bell pepper)
1 bunch watercress
1 cup pickled ginger
1 tablespoon black sesame seeds
1 cup coriander (cilantro) leaves
1 cup bean sprouts
250 ml (8 fl oz) canola oil
pinch of sea salt

Serves 4

Clean octopuses by peeling off skin and removing heads.
Grind toasted coriander seeds in a mortar and pestle.
Combine coriander, minced garlic, lemon juice, and sweet chilli sauce
in bowl. Add octopus and marinate in refrigerator for 2 hours.

Using a vegetable peeler, peel thin strips of cucumber. Thinly slice
bell pepper lengthwise. Combine watercress, cucumber, bell pepper,
pickled ginger, sesame seeds, cilantro leaves and bean sprouts in a
large bowl. Set aside.

Heat oil in a heavy-based skillet and fry sliced garlic until
golden brown and crispy. Remove and drain on a paper towel.
Strain marinade from the octopus into a small saucepan and bring to
simmer. Set aside to cool and use as dressing later.

Heat a wok and stir-fry octopus until cooked, approximately
3–4 minutes. Combine prepared salad with octopus and toss with
dressing. Season to taste.

CAESAR SALAD

1 clove garlic, peeled
1 teaspoon salt
1 teaspoon dry mustard
1 tablespoon lemon juice
¼ teaspoon Tabasco sauce
3 tablespoons olive oil
1 cos (romaine) lettuce, leaves washed and dried
1 endive, leaves washed and dried
2 tablespoons Parmesan cheese, grated
4 anchovy fillets, chopped into 3–4 pieces
1 coddled egg (boiled for 1 minute)
Garlic-infused croûtons, to serve (see page 27)

Serves 6–8

Rub salad bowl with cut clove of garlic. Put salt, mustard, lemon juice and Tabasco sauce into bowl and stir with wooden spoon until salt dissolves. Add olive oil and blend well.

Tear salad greens into bite-sized pieces and place in salad bowl. Sprinkle with grated cheese and add anchovy fillets. Break in the coddled egg and toss well, until all ingredients are well coated with dressing.

Just before serving, sprinkle with garlic-infused croûtons and toss again.

CALAMARI SALAD WITH BASIL DRESSING

300 g (10 oz) calamari
   tubes, washed
   and sliced into
   1 cm (½ in) rings
250 ml (8 fl oz) water
80 ml (2⅔ fl oz)
   lemon juice
80 ml (2⅔ fl oz)
   grapeseed oil
150 g (5 oz) snow peas,
   trimmed
100 g (3½ oz)
   button mushrooms
1 punnet cherry tomatoes
Serves 2

1 green capsicum
   (bell pepper),
   seeds and pith removed
   and cut into strips
2 tablespoons chives,
   chopped

BASIL DRESSING
60 ml (2 fl oz)
   French dressing
   (see page 360)
½ cup chopped fresh basil

Cook calamari in simmering water for 2 minutes or until
cooked. Drain.

Combine lemon juice and grapeseed oil. Pour mixture into a
bowl and add calamari. Toss calamari until coated. Cover bowl with
cling wrap and refrigerate overnight.

Place snow peas, mushrooms, tomatoes, capsicum and chives
into a salad bowl.

Drain calamari, reserving marinade. Add calamari to salad and
chill for 30 minutes, covered. In a bowl or jar, combine dressing
ingredients and reserved marinade. Chill for 30 minutes.

Just before serving, drizzle dressing over salad and toss lightly.

AVOCADO ORANGE SALAD

1 mignonette lettuce,
  washed and
  leaves separated
2 avocados, peeled,
  stoned and sliced
2 oranges, cut
  into segments
2 tablespoons slivered
  almonds, toasted

DRESSING
2 tablespoons
  orange juice
2 tablespoons olive oil
1 tablespoon white vinegar
1 teaspoon shallots
  (scallions), chopped
$\frac{1}{4}$ teaspoon curry powder
salt and ground black
  pepper, to taste

Serves 4

To make dressing, combine ingredients and season to taste.

Line a salad bowl with lettuce leaves. Layer remaining leaves into bowl. Arrange avocados and orange segments decoratively over lettuce. Drizzle dressing onto salad, and sprinkle with almonds.

COLESLAW

½ small cabbage, shredded
2 carrots, grated
1 onion, grated
1 clove garlic, crushed (optional)
⅔ stalk celery, sliced
2 tablespoons olive oil
125 ml (4 fl oz) mayonnaise (see page 367)
1 teaspoon salt
freshly ground black pepper, to taste
pinch of caster (superfine) sugar

Serves 4–6

Mix cabbage, carrots, onion, garlic and celery in a large salad bowl.
Combine olive oil, mayonnaise, salt and pepper and sugar in a separate bowl. Stir dressing through salad and serve immediately.

BEAN AND BREAD SALAD

cooking oil spray
12 slices crusty Italian bread
½ teaspoon cracked black pepper
½ teaspoon dried oregano
300 g (10 oz) canned borlotti beans, drained
12 cherry tomatoes, halved
¼ cup pitted black olives, halved
1 small red onion, sliced
¼ cup fresh basil leaves, chopped
1 tablespoon balsamic vinegar
baby cos lettuce leaves to serve
1 cup fresh basil leaves to garnish

Serves 4

Preheat oven to 180°C/360°F. Lightly spray bread slices on both sides with oil and place on an oven tray. Sprinkle one side of each bread slice with pepper and oregano and bake for 8 minutes, or until lightly browned and crisp.

Combine borlotti beans, tomatoes, olives, red onion, basil and vinegar in a large bowl and mix well. Arrange lettuce leaves on a serving plate with bean mixture and toasted bread. Serve garnished with fresh basil leaves.

CHINESE EGG NOODLES SALAD WITH CHICKEN

1 double breast of chicken,
    thinly sliced
1 tablespoon sesame oil
1/2 Chinese cabbage, sliced
1/2 cup slivered almonds
100 g (3½ oz) Chinese
    fried egg noodles,
    cooked
4 shallots (scallions),
    finely chopped
2 tomatoes, finely chopped

DRESSING
125 ml (4 fl oz) olive oil
125 ml (4 fl oz) balsamic
    vinegar
60 g (2 oz) caster
    (superfine) sugar
pinch of salt
2 tablespoons soy sauce

Serves 6–8

Heat oil in a frying pan and fry chicken. Set aside to cool.

To make dressing, combine all ingredients in a bowl (or jar) and mix well (or put the lid on and shake).

To serve, place chicken, Chinese cabbage, almonds, egg noodles, shallots and tomatoes in a bowl. Toss to combine, pour over dressing and serve immediately.

CUCUMBER SALAD

3 cucumbers, washed, dried and thinly sliced
1 tablespoon salt
2 cloves garlic, cut into slivers
180 ml (6 fl oz) balsamic vinegar
2 tablespoons sugar
freshly ground white pepper
1 tablespoon parsley, chopped, or fresh dill, to garnish

Serves 6–8

Arrange cucumber slices in a deep bowl and sprinkle with salt.
Cover with a small plate that fits inside the bowl and place a heavy
weight on top. Let this stand at room temperature for 2 hours.

Place garlic slivers in vinegar and let stand for at least
30 minutes.

Drain away juice from cucumber completely; squeeze cucumber
as dry as possible. Add sugar and pepper to garlic-infused vinegar
and pour over cucumber. Taste and adjust seasonings if necessary.
Cover tightly and chill thoroughly.

Before serving, drain off vinegar and sprinkle cucumber salad
with chopped parsley or dill.

LAMB SALAD

90 g (3 oz) cracked wheat
185 ml (6 fl oz) hot water
1 teaspoon butter
$\frac{1}{2}$ teaspoon ground tarragon
1 chicken stock cube, crumbled
$\frac{1}{2}$ teaspoon curry powder
$1\frac{1}{2}$ teaspoons dry mustard
$\frac{1}{2}$ teaspoon cayenne pepper
250 g ($\frac{1}{2}$ lb) cooked lamb, diced
1 onion, finely chopped
$\frac{1}{2}$ cup celery, sliced
2 tablespoons natural yogurt
2 tablespoons mayonnaise
lettuce cups, for serving
2 hard-boiled eggs, sliced, to garnish
parsley sprigs, to garnish

Serves 4–6

Combine wheat, water, butter, ground tarragon, stock cube,
curry powder, dry mustard and cayenne in a saucepan and heat,
stirring, until the mixture boils. Reduce heat, cover, and simmer for
10 minutes, or until all liquid is absorbed. Cool.

Add lamb, onion, celery, yogurt and mayonnaise, and toss well.
Chill for 30 minutes before serving.

To serve, spoon salad into lettuce cups, and garnish with egg
slices and parsley.

CRAB SALAD

400 g (14 oz) crabmeat, fresh or canned
4 crisp celery sticks, finely chopped
125 ml (4 fl oz) French dressing (see page 360)
salt and freshly ground black pepper, to taste
4 small butter lettuces, shredded
4 sprigs chives, to garnish

Serves 4

In a mixing bowl, combine crabmeat and celery. Moisten with
French dressing and salt and pepper and mix well.

Line a salad bowl with the shredded lettuce. Pile the crab on top.

Add some more dressing, scatter with chives just before serving.

LAMB WITH SESAME SEEDS SALAD

60 ml (2 fl oz) sesame oil
2 cloves garlic, finely chopped
200 g (6½ oz) lamb loin, seasoned with salt
    and freshly ground black pepper
mixed lettuce leaves
50 g (1⅔ oz) sesame seeds
freshly ground black pepper, to taste
100 ml (3 fl oz) lamb or veal stock
4 teaspoons sherry vinegar

Serves 2

In a heavy frying pan, heat oil and sauté garlic and seasoned lamb. Cook to your taste. Remove lamb from pan and slice into strips.

To serve, place lettuce on serving dish, top with lamb strips and sprinkle over sesame seeds and pepper. Deglaze pan with stock and vinegar and pour sauce over salad.

MEDITERRANEAN CHICKEN PASTA SALAD

1.5 kg (3 lb)
  chicken thighs
200 g (6½ oz)
  pasta twirls
100 g (3⅓ oz) pesto
200 g (6⅔ oz) sun-dried
  tomatoes in oil, sliced
200 g (6⅔ oz) snow peas,
  blanched and sliced
10 small mushrooms,
  sliced

¼ stick of celery, sliced
2 tablespoons
  balsamic vinegar
salt and freshly ground
  black pepper, to taste
1 lettuce (use your
  favorite variety),
  washed and leaves torn

Serves 6

Boil the chicken, and allow to cool. De-bone and cut up into bite-sized pieces.

Boil pasta for 8 minutes (in chicken stock if you wish, but it makes little difference to the dish), then rinse in cool water and drain. While pasta is warm, stir in pesto and sun-dried tomatoes and their oil.

Stir snow peas, mushrooms and celery into pasta, then add chicken. Sprinkle over balsamic vinegar and stir in, then season with salt and pepper. Let the dish sit for a few hours in the refrigerator, if possible.

When serving, put a layer of leaves on each plate first, then top with the chicken and pasta mix.

Note: You can use a mixture of types of lettuce (or other succulent leaves), which will improve the look and taste of the dish by giving it a range of colors, shapes and flavors. You can also add capsicum, or other mild herbs, but try to avoid strong flavors, such as onions or shallots.

LOBSTER SALAD

2 medium-sized lobsters, cooked
4 lettuce cups
150 ml (5 fl oz) mayonnaise
2 lemons, juiced
2 tomatoes, sliced
½ avocado, sliced
parsley, finely chopped

Serves 4

Crack the lobster claws with a light weight. If you have special
lobster picks, leave the meat in the cracked shells, otherwise
carefully take out the meat with a fine skewer. If leaving the
meat in the claws, arrange these beside the body of the lobster.
Remove meat from the shell, dice and place back in the shell.
If removing the meat from the claws, blend it with the body meat.
    Arrange lobster on lettuce, and top with some mayonnaise.
Mix together the lemon juice, tomatoes, avocado and parsley and
serve on the side.

CHICKEN & AVOCADO SALAD

3 skinless chicken breasts, cooked and sliced
1 small head of cos (romaine) lettuce, shredded
1 large red onion, thinly sliced
125 ml (4 fl oz) extra-virgin olive oil
60 ml (2 fl oz) red wine vinegar
salt and freshly ground black pepper
2 avocados, peeled and sliced

Serves 4

Place chicken, lettuce, and onion in a bowl. Thoroughly combine oil and vinegar, and season to taste with salt and pepper.

Pour over salad, toss gently, then arrange chicken on a serving plate. Garnish with avocado and serve.

INSALATA CAPRESE

400 g (1 lb) Roma tomatoes, thickly sliced
250 g (8 oz) bocconcini/fresh mozzarella, sliced
½ bunch fresh basil leaves, shredded
125 ml (4 fl oz) cup extra-virgin olive oil
2 tablespoons balsamic vinegar
sea salt and freshly ground black pepper

Serves 4

Arrange tomatoes, bocconcini, and basil leaves on individual plates.
   Drizzle with olive oil and balsamic vinegar, and sprinkle with sea salt and freshly ground black pepper.
   Serve with crusty bread.

POTATO SALAD

1 kg (2 lb) potatoes, peeled
75 ml (1½ fl oz) French dressing (see page 360)
½ cup cucumber, finely chopped
½ cup celery, finely chopped
¼ cup onion, finely sliced
4 hard-boiled eggs, coarsely chopped
250 ml (8 fl oz) mayonnaise
125 g (4 fl oz) sour cream
1 tablespoon horseradish relish
salt and freshly ground black pepper, to taste
2 rashers bacon, cooked and finely chopped, to garnish

Serves 6–8

Cook potatoes in boiling salted water until just tender. Drain well and leave to cool just enough to be handled, then cut into small cubes.

Place potato in a bowl and pour over French dressing, while potatoes are still warm. Let potatoes cool, then add cucumber, celery, onion and egg.

In a bowl, combine mayonnaise, sour cream and horseradish relish. Pour over potatoes and toss gently. Season with salt and pepper.

Garnish with bacon just before serving.

PASTA SALAD

500 g (1 lb) cooked spiral noodles
1 tablespoon olive oil
½ teaspoon salt
½ red capsicum (bell pepper),
    seeds and pith removed and diced
4–6 mushrooms, sliced
4–6 shallots (scallions), finely chopped
125 g (4 oz) mung beans
125 g (4 oz) corn kernels (optional)
300 ml (10 fl oz) mayonnaise

Serves 6–8

Place pasta into a large saucepan of boiling water with oil and salt,
and cook for 8 minutes or until pasta is al dente. Rinse and strain.
    Place all ingredients except dressing in a bowl and toss to
combine. Add dressing to taste.

SPANISH POTATO SALAD

1 tablespoon olive oil
1 tablespoon vinegar
salt and freshly ground black pepper, to taste
650 g (1½ lb) hot cooked potatoes, diced
125 g (4 oz) black olives or green and black combined
2 hard-boiled eggs
150 g (5 oz) celery, sliced or cucumber, diced
¼ cup pickled cucumber, diced
¼ cup green capsicum (bell pepper), seeds and pith
   removed and diced
80 g (2⅔ oz) mayonnaise
1 teaspoon onion, chopped

Serves 6–8

In a screw-top jar or small bowl, blend oil, vinegar, salt and pepper.
Pour over hot potatoes, toss lightly and allow to cool.
   Cut olives into quarters. Cut eggs lengthwise and
slice horizontally.
   Combine cooled potatoes, olives, eggs, celery, pickled cucumber
and green capsicum. In a cup, blend mayonnaise and onion. Mix this
lightly into salad. Chill well before serving.

SEAFOOD SALAD

1 small crayfish or 500 g (1 lb) shrimp,
    shelled, deveined and cooked
12 scallops, poached in white wine and drained
250 g (8 oz) white fish fillets, poached and flaked
250 ml (8 fl oz) French dressing
1 tablespoon lemon juice
250 ml (8 fl oz) sour cream or mayonnaise
125 ml (4 fl oz) tomato ketchup
1 cup celery, finely sliced
1 head lettuce, washed and finely shredded
12–16 plump oysters, chilled
parsley, chopped, to garnish

Serves 6

Remove flesh from crayfish body and legs, and cut into cubes. In a
bowl, combine crayfish or shrimp, scallops and fish. Pour French
dressing and lemon juice over seafood, then cover bowl and
marinate for 1 hour in the refrigerator.

Drain excess French dressing. In a small bowl, mix sour cream
with tomato ketchup and celery and fold through seafood.

Spoon seafood and sauce on a bed of finely shredded lettuce in
chilled individual bowls. Top with chilled oysters and sprinkle with
finely chopped parsley.

THAI BEEF SALAD

6 lettuce leaves
500 g (1 lb) beef rump or
   tenderloin, roasted and
   sliced into strips
2 cloves garlic,
   finely chopped
1 Spanish onion, sliced
1 stalk lemongrass
¼ cup coriander (cilantro)
   leaves, torn
1 cup mint leaves, torn
fried onion, to garnish
1 tablespoon dried chilli
   flakes, to garnish

DRESSING
4 kaffir lime leaves,
   cut into strips
3 cloves garlic,
   finely chopped
5 green chillies, seeded
   and finely chopped
1 tablespoon fish sauce
juice of 1 lime
50 g (1²/₃ oz) palm sugar
   or brown sugar

Serves 6

To make the salad dressing, combine all ingredients in a bowl
(or jar) and mix well (or put lid on and shake).

   To serve, arrange lettuce leaves on a serving dish, covering the
whole surface area. Place strips of beef over lettuce and sprinkle
over garlic, onion, lemongrass, coriander and mint.

   Pour the dressing over the top and garnish with fried onion
and chilli flakes.

WALDORF SALAD

1 green apple
1 red apple
juice of ½ lemon
1 cup celery, finely chopped
½ cup walnuts, chopped
60 g (2 oz) mayonnaise
crisp lettuce cups
1 red apple, thinly sliced, brushed with lemon juice
    to prevent discoloration, to garnish

Serves 6–8

Chill apples, then core and dice them. Pour lemon juice over apples.
Add celery, walnuts and mayonnaise and combine.
    Serve piled into lettuce cups and garnish with slices of
red apple.

LIGHT MEALS & SNACKS

BACON-WRAPPED SHRIMP

500 g (1 lb) shrimp, peeled and deveined
6–8 rashers bacon, rind removed and rashers halved
bamboo skewers, soaked in water
60 g (2 oz) butter, melted
60 ml (2 fl oz) lemon juice

Serves 6

Wrap each shrimp in a piece of bacon and thread onto bamboo skewers. In a small bowl or jug, combine melted butter and lemon juice. Brush over kebabs.

Grill kebabs over hot coals for approximately 10–15 minutes, or until shrimp is cooked and bacon is lightly brown and crisp. Turn frequently while cooking, and brush again with the melted butter and lemon juice before serving. Serve any remaining butter with the kebabs.

BAKED POTATOES

4 medium potatoes
1 head of garlic
2 rosemary sprigs

Serves 4

Preheat oven to 200°C (400°F). Scrub potatoes under running water and prick once with a skewer or a fork. This stops them exploding in the oven. Add the head of garlic and the rosemary. Put potatoes at the back of the centre shelf in the oven and bake for 1½ hours.

Remove potatoes from the oven and, using oven gloves, immediately break them in half. If you leave them whole, the skin goes wrinkly and soft.

Serve with butter or sour cream.

Note: Do not turn the oven down at all while the potatoes are cooking – they will go soft immediately.

BARBECUED CHICKEN DRUMSTICKS

12 chicken drumsticks

MARINADE
60 ml (2 fl oz) tomato sauce
2–3 tablespoons lemon juice
2 tablespoons soy sauce
60 ml (2 fl oz) olive oil
$1/2$ teaspoon salt

Serves 6

Grill chicken drumsticks over medium coals, turning frequently and basting with the marinade while cooking. Cook until drumsticks are tender.

To make the marinade, combine marinade ingredients in a large bowl and mix together well. Put chicken drumsticks into the bowl, cover and let stand for at least 20 minutes in the refrigerator.

BARBECUED SPARE RIBS

1 clove garlic, crushed
salt and black pepper, to taste
pinch of salt
1 tablespoon brown sugar
1 teaspoon paprika
1 teaspoon dry mustard
8 pork spare ribs
barbecue sauce, for serving

Serves 8

In a bowl, combine garlic, salt and pepper, salt, sugar, paprika and mustard. Rub spare ribs with this seasoning.

Grill spare ribs over medium coals, turning frequently and basting with the barbecue sauce while cooking. Cook for 15–20 minutes, or until spare ribs are tender.

Serve with baked potatoes and coleslaw (see pages 50 and 77).

BOILED EGGS

2 eggs

Serves 1

Place eggs in boiling water for 3 minutes for soft-boiled eggs and 6 minutes for hard-boiled eggs. Put eggs into cold water after cooking to cool slightly. This helps to remove shell easily.

POACHED EGGS ON TOAST

4 large eggs
2 slices sourdough bread, about 2 cm (¾ in) thick
75 ml (2½ fl oz) beetroot chutney
50 g (1¾ oz) rocket (arugula) leaves

Serves 2

Bring a medium saucepan of water to a simmer. Using a spoon, create a whirlpool and crack the eggs one at a time into the centre. Poach for about 3 minutes, or until the whites are slightly firm.

Toast the bread until golden brown. Arrange the toast, eggs, rocket and chutney onto two serving plates.

SCRAMBLED EGGS

8 eggs
160 ml (5½ fl oz) milk
salt and freshly ground black pepper
30 g (1 oz) butter

Serves 2

Beat the eggs lightly and add the milk, salt and pepper.

Heat the butter in a frying pan, add the beaten eggs and stir continuously with a wooden spoon until a creamy texture. Do not have the heat too high.

BAKED EGGS

100 g (3½ oz) spinach leaves, coarsely chopped
50 g (1¾ oz) salted ricotta, sliced
60 ml (2 fl oz) thickened cream
2 large eggs

Serves 2

Preheat the oven to 190°C (375°F). Place two ramekins in a deep baking tray.

Wash the spinach and place in a medium saucepan and cook over low heat until wilted, 2 minutes. Drain the excess water. Transfer the spinach to a medium bowl. Add the ricotta and cream and stir to combine. Spoon the spinach mixture into the ramekins and break an egg into the centre.

Fill the baking tray with boiling water to come halfway up the sides of the ramekins. Bake in the oven for 15 minutes, or until the eggs have set.

THE OMELET

No one comes into this world as an instinctive maker of omelets. The omelet needs much more than the breaking of eggs and the application of heat – it can be the easiest, and also the trickiest process. The choice of pan, of eggs, and of butter must be considered, as well as the time and desire to practice. An omelet is similar to scrambled eggs, but is folded in the pan when just set and ready to turn out, and can be varied by the addition of a filling. The filling adds interest, but plays the minor role in the cooking process.

THE BASIC OMELET

3 large eggs
salt and freshly ground black pepper, to taste
1 tablespoon water
15 g (½ oz) butter

Serves 1

Place a pan over low heat and warm slowly. Break eggs into a bowl, add salt and pepper, and water. Beat ingredients with a large fork to mix well, but no more. Over-beaten eggs can become watery.

Raise heat under omelet pan, and add butter. When this begins to show a faint brown color, pour in eggs. Using a fork, and holding the pan with your hand, stir the mixture in the centre a few times, and bring the eggs from the side of the pan towards the middle. This enables any uncooked liquid to run to the sides and cook more easily. As soon as the underside is a light golden brown, and the centre is creamy, lift the edge of the omelet nearest the pan handle, fold the omelet in half and gently roll it towards the edge.

To turn omelet out, hold the omelet pan with your left hand underneath the handle, turn over with a quick flick of the wrist and flip the omelet onto a warmed plate.

If a filling is to be added, make it beforehand and keep it hot, then spread it on half the cooked surface and fold the side of the omelet with no filling over it. In some cases, as with chopped herbs, the filling is cooked with the egg mixture.

FRIED EGGS

2 **eggs**
1 tablespoon olive oil, for frying

Serves 1

Warm frying pan, adding oil to cover the surface. Put egg rings in the frying pan and crack eggs into them. Cook on a low heat for 2 minutes for sunny side up; flip eggs and cook for another minute if you prefer easy over eggs.

Serve hot with buttered toast.

CINNAMON TOAST

125 g (4 oz) caster (superfine) sugar
2–3 teaspoons ground cinnamon
6 slices white bread
butter, softened

Serves 3

Mix sugar and cinnamon in a bowl.

Toast the bread lightly on both sides and butter one side, spreading the butter right to the edges. Using a spoon, sprinkle each slice of toast evenly with the cinnamon and sugar mixture. Put the toast under the grill and cook until the sugar starts to melt. Remove and serve hot.

FRENCH TOAST

3–4 eggs
125 ml (4 fl oz) milk
2 tablespoons caster (superfine) sugar
¼ teaspoon vanilla essence
pinch of salt
butter, for frying
8 thick slices of bread

Serves 4

In a large bowl, combine eggs, milk, sugar, vanilla and salt.

Heat a little butter in a frying pan over medium heat. Dip a slice of bread into the egg mixture until bread is completely coated and has soaked up some egg mixture. Place bread in the frying pan and cook for 1 minute on each side, or until it is crisp and golden. Repeat with remaining bread, until egg mixture has all been used.

Serve hot with maple syrup, bacon and fried or raw banana.

CRUMBED CALAMARI RINGS

750 g (1½ lb) squid tubes (squid hoods)
260 g (9 oz) plain (all-purpose) flour
sea salt and pepper
2–3 eggs
60 ml (2 fl oz) milk
120 g (4 oz) panko breadcrumbs
oil, for deep-frying
lemon wedges, to serve

Serves 6

Cut squid tubes into 5 mm (¼ inch) rings. Place the rings on absorbent paper and dry well.

Sift plain flour into a bowl and season with salt and pepper.

Whisk eggs and milk together in a shallow bowl.

Toss the squid rings into the flour, one at a time, then dip into the egg mixture, shaking off any extra liquid. Toss rings in panko breadcrumbs to coat.

Heat oil to medium-high heat (it may spit and splatter, so be careful). Cook the rings in the hot oil until golden brown (3 minutes maximum). Drain well and serve hot with lemon wedges.

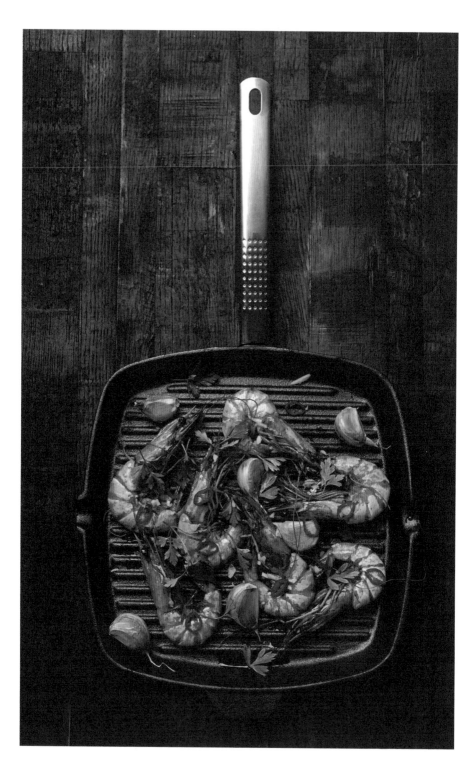

GRILLED SHRIMP

1 kg (2 lb) green shrimp, peeled and deveined

MARINADE
250 ml (8 fl oz) olive oil
60 ml (2 fl oz) lemon juice
75g (2½ oz) onion, finely chopped
2 cloves garlic, crushed
 parsley, finely chopped

Serves 4

To make marinade, place all marinade ingredients in a large bowl
and mix well. Add shrimp to the bowl and combine. Cover bowl and
let stand for several hours in the refrigerator. Drain shrimp.

Place shrimp in a heavy-based frying pan or skillet and
cook over medium coals for 10–15 minutes, or until cooked.
Stir frequently and add a little marinade while cooking.
Serve immediately.

CHEESE SOUFFLÉ

60 g (2 oz) butter
1 tablespoon fresh white breadcrumbs
75 g (2½ oz) Parmesan cheese, grated
3 tablespoons plain (all-purpose) flour
280 ml (9 fl oz) milk
4 egg yolks
¾ teaspoon salt
¼ teaspoon ground black pepper
pinch of cayenne pepper
¼ teaspoon paprika
30 g (1 oz) Gruyère cheese, grated
5 egg whites

Serves 4

Preheat oven to 200°C (400°F). Grease the inside of a 15 cm (6 in) soufflé dish with 15 g (½ oz) butter, then sprinkle with breadcrumbs and 1 tablespoon Parmesan cheese. Cut a band of greaseproof paper about 18 cm (7 in) wide (it needs to stick up 5 cm (2 in) higher than the top of the dish), and long enough to go round the outside of the dish. Fold the paper in half lengthways and butter the top half of one side of it. Tie the paper round the soufflé dish with string, with the butter side on the inside, sticking up beyond the dish.

Melt remaining butter in a saucepan, stir in flour and cook over a gentle heat for about 1 minute. Add milk and stir continuously over a moderate heat until mixture thickens and boils. Simmer for 5 seconds. Remove from heat, add egg yolks one at a time, beating in well. Add seasonings, remaining Parmesan cheese and Gruyère cheese.

Whisk egg whites until they form stiff, firm peaks. Stir a heaped tablespoon of egg white into the sauce to lighten it, then gently fold in the remaining egg whites. Pour soufflé mixture into soufflé dish. Bake on middle shelf of the oven for 30–40 minutes. Serve immediately.

CHICKEN SATAY STICKS

185 g (6 oz) chicken
few drops soy sauce
few drops of Tabasco sauce
1 teaspoon white vinegar
1 teaspoon oil
1 teaspoon brown sugar
1 clove garlic
bamboo skewers, soaked in water

Serves 2

Cut chicken into 1.25 cm (½ in) cubes, leaving the fat on. In a bowl, combine soy sauce, Tabasco sauce, white vinegar, oil, brown sugar and garlic. Put chicken cubes into bowl and marinate for at least 2 hours in the refrigerator.

Put chicken cubes on skewers and grill very quickly under a hot grill. Serve on the skewers accompanied by a bed of rice.

LAMB KEBABS

1 x 2 kg (4½ lb) leg of lamb
500 g (1 lb) small onions
1 green or yellow capsicum (bell pepper), pith and
seeds removed
6 bamboo skewers
6 small tomatoes
bay leaves (optional)
salt and freshly ground black pepper, to taste
olive oil or melted butter

Serves 6

Soak the bamboo skewers in water for 10 minutes prior to use.

Cut lamb into 2.5 cm (1 in) cubes. Peel onions and blanch in boiling water, then drain. Cut capsicum and bacon into 2.5 cm (1 in) pieces.

Thread lamb onto skewers alternately with onion, capsicum and tomatoes. Small bay leaves can be added if used. Season with salt and pepper and brush with oil. Grill gently, turning and brushing again with oil if necessary, for 20–25 minutes, or until meat is cooked.

Serve on a bed of rice or with salad.

CORN ON THE COB

4 ears of corn on the cob
30 g (1 oz) butter
salt and freshly ground black pepper, to taste

Serves 4

Turn back husks of the corn and strip off silk. Brush corn with melted butter or margarine and sprinkle with salt and freshly ground black pepper. Replace the husks and secure in three places with string.

Barbecue corn cobs over hot coals for 15–20 minutes, or until tender, turning frequently. When cooked, husks will be dry and brown and corn will be golden brown. Serve with melted butter and salt and pepper.

Variation: After stripping off silk, wrap a bacon rasher (remove rind first) around each corn cob and secure at the ends with cocktail sticks. Replace the husks and proceed as above.

Note: Select young, tender corn cobs by checking they are a bright yellow in color and not wrinkled. You can remove husks from corn cobs completely. If you do this, brush corn with melted butter and season with salt and pepper, then wrap each corn cob in aluminum foil and barbecue over hot coals for 20 minutes, or until tender. Serve as above.

GRILLED LAMB CUTLETS

6 lamb cutlets
salt and freshly ground black pepper, to taste
olive oil for frying

Serves 2

Trim cutlets of excess fat and season well on each side. Put on rack in grill pan, and brush with oil. Cook under a very hot grill for 2 minutes to sear meat. Turn and sear other side for 2 minutes. Move the grill pan down and cook for a further 10 minutes (turning once after 5 minutes), or until cooked.

Serve with salad or vegetables.

CRUMBED LAMB CUTLETS

8 lamb cutlets
lemon juice, to taste (optional)
salt and freshly ground black pepper, to taste
plain (all-purpose) flour, for coating
1 egg, beaten with 1 tablespoon of water
breadcrumbs, for coating
olive oil, for frying
parsley, chopped, to garnish

Serves 4

Trim skin and excess fat from cutlets and flatten with the side of a meat mallet (unless your butcher has already done this). Lay cutlets on a plate, sprinkle with a little lemon juice (if using) and season with salt and pepper. Let cutlets stand in refrigerator for 1 hour. To finish cutlets, coat with flour then dip in beaten egg and finally breadcrumbs, pressing them on firmly.

Pour enough oil to be 5 mm (¼ in) deep in a heavy frying pan and heat. Fry cutlets over a moderate heat for 4–5 minutes on either side, then lift them out and drain them on absorbent paper.

Serve immediately, while still crisp and piping hot, garnished with parsley.

Variations:

- Parsley Cutlets: to each 30 g (1 oz) breadcrumbs, add 2 tablespoons finely chopped parsley.
- Parmesan Cutlets: to each 30 g (1 oz) breadcrumbs, add 2 tablespoons grated Parmesan cheese.
- Rosemary Cutlets: to each 30 g (1 oz) breadcrumbs add ¼ teaspoon powdered or ½ teaspoon dried spikes of rosemary.

DOLMADES
(STUFFED VINE LEAVES)

16 fresh or tinned vine leaves
500 g (1 lb) lean minced (ground) beef
220 g (7 oz) long grain rice
2 onions, finely chopped
1 clove garlic, crushed
2 teaspoons salt
½ teaspoon freshly ground black pepper
1 teaspoon dried oregano leaves
1 tablespoon fresh mint, chopped
625 ml (21 fl oz) beef stock (see page 376)

Serves 4

If using fresh vine leaves, choose medium-sized leaves that are not too dark in color. Large, dark leaves are tough. Snip off stems with kitchen scissors, wash well, place in a bowl and pour boiling water over to soften. If using tinned vine leaves in brine, wash in warm water before filling.

To prepare meat filling, combine all remaining ingredients except stock in a bowl, mixing thoroughly. Divide mixture into 16 portions and shape into small sausage shapes. On a wooden board, arrange one leaf at a time, shiny side down, and place a portion of filling on the leaf, near the stem. Fold over top of leaf, then sides. Roll up, enclosing meat completely.

Pack rolls close together, in neat rows, in a heavy saucepan. If necessary, put a second layer on top of the first. Pour stock into the saucepan and cover with lid. Bring slowly to a simmer and cook gently for 45 minutes to 1 hour. Serve hot.

FISHCAKES

250 g (8 oz) white fish, poached or steamed
250 g (8 oz) mashed potatoes
1 egg
salt and freshly ground black pepper, to taste
30–60 g (1–2 oz) butter for frying
parsley and lemon, to garnish

COATING
15–30 g ($\frac{1}{2}$–1 oz) seasoned flour
1 egg, beaten
3–4 tablespoons crisp breadcrumbs

Serves 4

Remove all bones and skin from the fish, then flake with a fork.
In a bowl, place fish, potato, egg and seasoning. Mix well, then
divide into 8 round cakes.

Coat the fishcakes in seasoned flour, then egg, then
breadcrumbs.

Heat butter in a frying pan and fry fishcakes for 2–3 minutes,
until golden brown on the underside. Turn, then cook for the
same time on the second side. Lift out of pan and drain on
absorbent paper.

Serve hot, garnished with lemon.

FRIED ONION AND POTATO BALLS

4 large potatoes, washed and peeled
1 onion, chopped
1 tablespoon butter
60 g (2 oz) plain (all-purpose) wholemeal flour
salt and freshly ground black pepper, to taste
dash of milk
125 ml (4 fl oz) vegetable oil

Serves 4

Cook potatoes in boiling salted water until tender. Drain and place in a bowl.

Fry onion in butter until soft and golden.

Mash potatoes, then add flour, salt and pepper, fried onion and just enough milk to form a firm dough. Roll into small balls about 2.5 cm (1 in) in size.

Heat oil in a large frying pan and fry onion and potato balls until golden brown all over. Drain on absorbent paper and serve with a green salad.

FRIED OYSTERS

12 oysters
salt and freshly ground black pepper, to taste
1 egg yolk
60 ml (2 fl oz) milk
breadcrumbs, to coat
olive oil, for frying
chopped parsley, to garnish
lemon wedges

Serves 1–2

Remove oysters from shell and season with salt and pepper.
Set shells aside.

In a bowl, whisk egg yolk with milk. Dip oysters in mixture,
drain, then roll in breadcrumbs. Deep-fry in hot oil for 2 minutes.
Warm shells in oven and place fried oysters in them.

FRIED SHRIMP

2 shallots (scallions), finely chopped
3 slices fresh ginger
2 tablespoons dry sherry
1 teaspoon salt
1 tablespoon cornflour (cornstarch)
1 kg (2 lb) green shrimp, peeled and deveined
olive oil, for frying

Serves 4

In a bowl, combine shallots, ginger, sherry, salt and cornflour, and mix until smooth. Coat shrimp with the mixture.

In a large frying pan, heat oil until hot and fry shrimp for 3–5 minutes, depending on their size. You'll know the shrimp are cooked when their meat turns white. Serve immediately.

SEAFOOD FLAN

PASTRY CASE
500 g (1 lb) plain (all-
  purpose) flour
½ teaspoon salt
pinch of cayenne pepper
pinch of freshly ground
  black pepper
125 g (4 oz) butter
1 egg yolk
2 teaspoons lemon juice
4–6 teaspoons water

FILLING
15 g (½ oz) butter
1 small onion, chopped

3 eggs
1 extra egg yolk
125 ml (4 fl oz)
  fresh cream
salt and pepper, to taste
1 teaspoon lemon rind,
  finely grated
375 g (12 oz) mixed
  shellfish (shrimp, rock
  lobster, oysters and
  scallops)
2–3 tablespoons
  warm brandy

Serves 4–6

Preheat oven to 180°C (350°F). To make pastry, sift flour and seasonings into a bowl. Rub butter into flour with fingertips until mixture resembles breadcrumbs. In another bowl, mix egg yolk, lemon juice and water. Add this to flour and mix with a round-bladed knife to form a stiff dough. Cover with plastic film and place in the refrigerator for 30 minutes.

On a floured surface, roll out pastry and line a 23 cm (9 in) flan tin with it. Prick base of flan, line inside with a circle of greased baking paper and sprinkle with dried beans or peas. Blind bake in the middle shelf of the oven for 15–20 minutes. Do not allow to brown. Remove pastry from oven and remove paper and beans.

To make filling, melt butter in a saucepan, add onion and sauté until soft. Do not let onion brown. In a bowl, whisk eggs, egg yolk, cream, seasonings and lemon rind together. Add to sautéed onion and mix. In another saucepan, heat seafood gently in brandy.

Place seafood in flan tin and gently pour over the egg mixture. Cook in the oven for 25–30 minutes, or until filling is set and golden brown. Serve immediately.

FRIED SCALLOPS

500 g (1 lb) scallops
flour seasoned with salt and black pepper
60 g (2 oz) self-raising flour
15 g (½ oz) butter, melted
125 ml (4 fl oz) lukewarm water
1 egg white
¼ teaspoon salt
pinch of paprika
olive oil, for frying
parsley sprigs, to garnish

Serves 4

To make batter: Sift flour into a bowl. Make a well in the centre and add butter and water. Beat together until a smooth batter is formed. Let stand until ready to use. Bater will keep in the refrigerator for 5-7 days. In another bowl, whisk egg white and salt together until stiff. Gently fold into batter and use immediately.
Roll scallops in seasoned flour, dip in batter and sprinkle with paprika . Deep-fry in hot oil for 1 minute, or until batter is golden. Drain scallops on paper toweling.
    Fry parsley sprigs in hot oil until crisp. Drain and serve with french fries and a green salad.

GARLIC BREAD

1 stick of French bread
2 cloves garlic, peeled and crushed
250 g (8 oz) butter

Serves 4

Preheat oven to 220°C (420°F). With a sharp knife, cut bread into slices almost to the bottom, being careful not to sever the slices.

In a small bowl, mash garlic thoroughly into butter. Spread garlic butter generously on both sides of bread slices. Wrap bread loosely in aluminum foil, place in the oven for 10–15 minutes, and bake until bread is crisp and golden. Serve hot.

GARLIC SHRIMP

125 ml (4 fl oz) olive oil
4 large cloves garlic, peeled
1 tablespoon parsley, chopped
$\frac{1}{2}$ teaspoon salt
1 kg (2 lb) small green shrimp peeled and deveined

Serves 12 as an appetizer, 8 as an entrée

In a bowl, combine oil, garlic, parsley and salt. Add shrimp and let stand for 2 hours covered in the refrigerator.

Preheat oven to 250°C (485°F). Place shrimp and marinade in an ovenproof casserole dish and cook in the oven for 10 minutes, or until shrimp turn pink. Remove garlic cloves.

Serve as an appetizer on small cocktail sticks, or as an entrée in small ramekins.

GLAZED ONIONS

500 g (1 lb) small onions
30 g (1 oz) butter
1 teaspoon brown sugar
salt and freshly ground black pepper, to taste

Serves 4

Peel onions and blanch for 5–7 minutes. Drain well. Put into a
saucepan with butter, sugar and seasoning. Cook gently with lid on,
shaking and stirring from time to time, until onions become tender
and well glazed. This should take 7–10 minutes. Make sure that the
cooking is slow, or the sugar will burn. Serve hot.

GUACAMOLE

2 tablespoons lemon juice
2–3 tablespoons olive oil
$\frac{1}{2}$ clove garlic, peeled and crushed
salt, to taste
$\frac{1}{2}$ teaspoon Tabasco sauce
2 large avocados, diced
2 heaped tablespoons sour cream
1 small onion, finely chopped
1 tomato, diced

Serves 8

Place all ingredients except onion and tomato in a bowl and
beat together with a fork until a smooth consistency is reached.
Add tomato and onion and mix through. Serve with corn chips.

HAMBURGERS

1 small onion, grated
500 g (1 lb) minced steak
3 tablespoons plain (all-purpose) flour
60 ml (2 fl oz) milk
125 g (4 oz) extra plain (all-purpose) flour
60 ml (2 fl oz) oil
6 hamburger buns
Tomato sauce

Serves 6

Mix onion and meat thoroughly in a bowl using a wooden spoon. Add flour and mix in thoroughly. Pour milk over meat mixture and stir in well.

Place extra flour in a small bowl. Make a heaped tablespoon of the meat mixture into a ball and roll it in the flour until it is well coated. Lift it out onto a plate and flatten it slightly. Continue until all the meat is used.

Pour oil into a frying pan and place over a medium heat. When the oil starts to bubble, gently place hamburger patties in the pan. Cook until the bottom of the hamburgers are brown, then flip them over and cook until they are brown on the other side. Drain patties on absorbent paper. (They can also be grilled or barbecued.)

Place patties on hamburger buns and add tomato sauce.

Variations: add sliced cheese, sliced cucumber, sliced tomatoes, sliced beetroot and lettuce – or salad ingredients of your choice.

HAM AND PINEAPPLE PIZZA

1 round piece Lebanese bread
3 tablespoons tomato paste or Italian Tomato Sauce
  (see page 366)
125 g (4 oz) mozzarella cheese, grated

HAM AND PINEAPPLE TOPPING
100 g (3½ oz) sliced ham
1 x 440 g (14 oz) can crushed pineapple

Serves 2

Preheat oven to 200°C (400°F). Place the bread on a pizza plate
or baking sheet. Using a knife, spread the bread very thinly with
the tomato paste. Sprinkle with half the cheese. This is the basic
pizza base.

Cut ham slices into pieces about 1 cm (½ in) square. Open the
can of pineapple and drain off juice. Place ham slices on top of
the cheese, then add pineapple pieces. Cover with the rest of
the cheese.

Cook in the oven until the cheese turns golden brown
(about 10 minutes) and serve.

MASHED POTATO

4 medium-sized potatoes, peeled
125 ml (4 fl oz) milk
30 g (1 oz) butter
60 g (2 oz) cheese, grated
salt and freshly ground black pepper, to taste

Serves 4

Place potatoes into a saucepan with cold, lightly salted water
to cover. Bring to the boil and cook gently, covered, for
20–30 minutes, until potatoes are easily pierced with a fork.
Drain thoroughly, then shake pan over heat for a minute or two until
all surplus moisture has evaporated and potatoes are dry.

Mash potatoes, then beat with a wooden spoon until very
smooth. In a saucepan, heat milk and butter. Once mixture is
hot, add potatoes and beat until light and fluffy. Add cheese
and stir through until melted. Season with salt and pepper.
Serve immediately.

FRENCH FRIES

6 large potatoes
300 ml (10½ fl oz) vegetable oil, for deep-frying
salt, to taste

Serves 2

Peel potatoes and cut into pieces 5 x 1 x 1 cm (2 x ½ x ½ in).
Place in a large bowl and cover with ice cold water for at least
30 minutes. Dry french fries thoroughly in a clean tea towel.

Heat oil until very hot – a 2.5 cm (1 in) cube of bread will
brown in 1 minute when the oil is hot enough. Place dry fries in a
frying basket and lower into the oil. The fries should be completely
covered by oil. Fry until tender but not browned, for about
10 minutes. Remove fries from oil and drain. Put chips aside until
just before serving time.

Reheat oil and cook fries until golden, crisp and slightly puffy.
Drain very well, sprinkle with salt, and serve immediately.

Variation: For potato straws, cut potatoes into matchstick-shaped
pieces, then prepare and fry as above.

MEAT PIE

2 tablespoons oil
1 kg (2 lb) chuck or
   skirt steak, cut into
   2.5 cm (1 in) cubes
2 onions, chopped
½ cup celery, chopped
½ cup carrot, chopped
500 ml (1 pint) beef stock
   (see page 376)
2 teaspoons salt

¼ teaspoon freshly
   ground black pepper
¼ teaspoon
   ground nutmeg
3 tablespoons plain
   (all-purpose) flour
185 g (6 oz) short crust
   pastry
1 egg, beaten, for glazing

Serves 8

Heat oil in a large saucepan and fry steak in about three lots until browned, then remove. Add onion, celery and carrot and cook for a few minutes. Replace meat, add stock, cover and simmer gently for 1 hour. Add salt, pepper and nutmeg and simmer for another hour, until cooked.

In a cup, blend flour with a little cold water to form a smooth paste. Add to saucepan and cook a little longer, until mixture thickens. Taste and adjust flavor.

Preheat oven to 200°C (400°F). Place a pie funnel in the centre of a large pie dish or large heavy frypan, then add meat to come to within 2 cm (1 in) of the top.

Roll out pastry on a lightly floured board, so that it is 2.5 cm (1 in) larger than the top of the pie dish. Cut a strip 1 cm (½ in) wide off the edge and place it on the dampened edge of the pie dish. Glaze this strip of pastry with egg, then lift remaining pastry on, easing it gently. (If you stretch it, it will shrink during cooking.) Press edges together, then trim combined edge and decorate with a knife. Glaze pastry with egg. Make a few holes in the pastry for steam to escape. Bake in the oven for 25 minutes, or until cooked.

POTATO CROQUETTES

500 g (1 lb) potatoes, peeled
30 g (1 oz) butter
1 egg yolk
2 tablespoons hot milk
salt and freshly ground black pepper, to taste
seasoned flour
2 eggs, beaten
breadcrumbs for coating
olive oil for frying

Serves 6

Cook potatoes in boiling, salted water until tender. Drain, then dry potatoes with a tea towel. Mash and press through a sieve or potato ricer. Return to pan. Add butter, egg yolk, milk, and salt and pepper, and beat until smooth. Divide mixture into small pieces similar to the shape of wine corks.

Roll croquettes in seasoned flour, then brush with egg and roll in breadcrumbs. Deep-fry in hot oil until golden brown.

MUSSELS WITH GARLIC

72 mussels in their shells, washed
1 L (2 pints) water
250 g (8 oz) butter
salt and freshly ground black pepper, to taste
2 cloves garlic, finely chopped
2 tablespoons parsley, chopped
fine dry breadcrumbs

Serves 6–8

Place mussels and water in a steamer and steam mussels open by shaking them over a high flame. Keep mussels in half shell and arrange on a platter.

In a saucepan, melt butter, then add salt and pepper, garlic and parsley. Drizzle butter over mussels. Sprinkle with breadcrumbs and place under a preheated hot grill until brown. Serve at once.

QUICHE

PASTRY
250 g (8 oz) self-raising
(self-rising) flour
185 g (6 oz) hard butter,
grated
1 egg yolk
60 ml (2 fl oz) cold milk

FILLING
625 ml (1 $\frac{1}{5}$ pint) milk
3 eggs
3 shallots (scallions),
chopped
125 g (4 oz) ham,
chopped
125 g (4 oz) cheese,
grated

Serves 4

Preheat oven to 200°C (400°F).

To make the pastry, sift flour into a large bowl and add butter. Mix with your fingertips until mixture resembles breadcrumbs. Use your fingertips to break up large lumps. Make a hollow in the centre and drop in the egg yolk. Mix again with your fingertips. Pour in milk, a little at a time, until you can make a ball of pastry that sticks together. On a floured surface, roll out the pastry until it is 5 mm (¼ in) thick. Place the pastry in a flan ring or pie dish and trim off the edges. Put it into the refrigerator, covered, for about 30 minutes.

To make the filling, pour milk into a large bowl, break eggs in and beat with an egg beater. Stir onion and ham into the mixture and pour into the pastry shell. Sprinkle cheese over the top and bake in the oven for 45 minutes, or until the quiche is set.

SALMON POTATO CAKES

1 kg (2 lb) boiled potatoes, peeled
60 g (2 oz) butter
freshly ground black pepper, to taste
2 hard-boiled eggs, chopped
250 g (8 oz) salmon, poached and flaked
salt and freshly ground black pepper, to taste
1 egg, beaten
fine breadcrumbs, for coating
olive oil, for frying

Serves 6

Mash potatoes with butter and pepper and divide into 24 small portions. Shape each portion into a small flat cake, about 5 mm (¼ in) thick.

Mix hard-boiled eggs and salmon in a bowl. Season with salt and pepper.

Place a spoonful of the salmon mixture on a potato cake and cover with another potato cake, pressing edges firmly together to seal. Dip each cake in beaten egg, then coat with breadcrumbs.

Fry in olive oil until golden brown, then drain on absorbent paper and serve immediately.

SALMON QUICHE

PASTRY
60 g (2 oz) white flour,
   sifted
60 g (2 oz)
   wholemeal flour
½ teaspoon salt
90 g (3 oz) butter
1 egg yolk
1 tablespoon lemon juice

FILLING
4 slices bacon, rind
   removed and diced
250 g (8 oz) tin salmon
   in brine

3 eggs
100 g spinach
375 ml (12 ½ fl oz)
   fresh cream
1 tablespoon parsley,
   chopped
1 tablespoon Parmesan
   cheese, grated
½ teaspoon paprika
1 teaspoon salt
freshly ground black
   pepper, to taste

Serves 6

Preheat oven to 200°C (400°F).

To make pastry, mix flours and salt together in a bowl. Rub in the butter with your fingertips, until the mixture resembles fine breadcrumbs. Add egg yolk and lemon juice and mix to form a firm dough (if necessary, add a tablespoon of water). Press the pastry into a 25 cm (10 in) flan tin.

To make filling, gently fry bacon in a small frying pan. Drain on absorbent paper. Drain and flake salmon, reserving liquid. Arrange the salmon on the base of the pastry, then sprinkle bacon on top.

In a bowl, beat together reserved salmon liquid, eggs, spinach, cream, parsley, cheese, paprika, salt and pepper. Pour mixture gently, over the back of a spoon, into the flan tin to cover salmon and bacon.

Bake in the oven for 10 minutes then reduce heat to 165°C (325°F) and cook a further 30–35 minutes, or until the filling is set.

TOMATO TOASTS WITH FRESH BASIL

4 tablespoons olive oil
1 teaspoon mixed dried herbs
freshly ground black pepper
1 baguette, cut into 12 slices
8 Roma or plum tomatoes
1 clove garlic, crushed
25 g (¾oz) sun-dried tomatoes in oil,
    drained and finely chopped
1 teaspoon vinegar
1 teaspoon sugar
2 tablespoons fresh basil, chopped

Serves 4

Preheat the oven to 220°C (430°F). Combine 3 tablespoons of the oil with the dried herbs and pepper and season well. Brush both sides of each bread slice with the flavored oil. Cook for 8 minutes or until lightly golden and crisp.

Meanwhile, put the tomatoes in a bowl, cover with boiling water and leave for 30 seconds. Peel and deseed, then roughly chop the flesh.

Heat the remaining olive oil in a frying pan and add the garlic, chopped tomatoes, sun-dried tomatoes, vinegar, sugar and basil. Cook, stirring occasionally, for 5 minutes or until heated through. Remove from the heat. Pile the tomato mixture on top of the toasts, season and serve.

SALMON SPREAD

10-15 slices smoked salmon
2 tablespoons dill, freshly chopped
freshly ground black pepper

SALMON SAUCE
3 tablespoons sweet mustard
1 tablespoon French mustard
1 egg yolk
2 tablespoons sugar
2 tablespoons white wine vinegar
200 ml (7 fl oz) olive oil

Serves 6-8

To make the sauce mix all sauce ingredients thoroughly.
Cut the salmon into thin shreds and bind it with the sauce.
Season with freshly ground pepper. Serve with crackers or
chunky slices of bread and garnish with flat-leaf parsley,
chopped chives or fresh dill.

CHICKEN LIVER PÂTÉ

1 onion, finely chopped
1 clove garlic, finely chopped
1 rasher bacon, finely chopped
125 g (4 oz) butter
250 g (8 oz) chicken livers, cleaned
½ teaspoon fresh thyme, chopped
salt and freshly ground black pepper
60 ml (2 fl oz) cream
1 tablespoon brandy
1 packet water crackers

Serves 4

Melt butter in a frypan, add the onion, garlic and bacon and cook until tender.

Add chicken livers, thyme, salt and pepper. Cook a further 5 minutes. Allow to cool slightly then place in a food processor and process until smooth.

Add brandy and cream and process until well combined.

Place into a large mold and chill. To serve place mold on a platter and surround with crackers.

SMOKED OYSTER DIP

125 g (4 oz) cream cheese
1 shallot (scallion),
   cut into 25 mm (1 in) lengths
1 teaspoon lemon juice
100 g (3½ oz) canned smoked oysters
salt and freshly ground black pepper
1 packet crackers

Serves 4

In a food processor, place cream cheese, shallot and lemon juice and beat until smooth, with shallot finely chopped.

Add smoked oysters with oil, directly from the can with salt and pepper. Pulse in 2 second bursts until oysters are roughly chopped.

Place in serving bowl, cover and refrigerate. Serve with a selection of crackers.

SHRIMP TOAST

10 green tiger shrimp, peeled
½ small garlic clove, crushed
1 teaspoon soy sauce, plus extra
1 teaspoon lemon juice
dash of Tabasco sauce
60 g (2 oz) sesame seeds, plus extra
8 slices white bread, crusts removed
oil for deep-frying

Makes 16 triangles

Purée the shrimps, garlic, soy sauce, lemon juice, Tabasco sauce and half the sesame seeds in a blender or food processor.

Spread mixture over one side of each slice of bread, sprinkle with a few sesame seeds, gently press down sesame seeds and cut bread diagonally, into triangles.

Heat oil for deep-frying in a saucepan or deep-fat fryer to 200°C (400°F), or until a cube of bread browns in 30 seconds. Cook the toasts a few at a time for about 3 minutes, until crisp and golden. Drain on absorbent paper and keep warm while cooking the remainder.

Put a small bowl of soy sauce for dipping in the centre of a large plate and arrange the toasts around and serve.

SATAY CHICKEN TRIANGLES

3 small chicken fillets,
diced
20 sheets filo pastry
butter, melted

MARINADE
60 ml (2 fl oz) oil
2 tablespoons white
wine vinegar
1 tablespoon
teriyaki sauce
2 teaspoons sesame oil

PEANUT SAUCE
1 tablespoon
tomato ketchup
2 teaspoons chilli sauce
125g (4 oz) smooth
peanut butter
80 ml (3 fl oz) chicken
stock
2 teaspoons lemon juice

Makes 30 triangles

To make marinade, combine all marinade ingredients in a bowl.
Add chicken and marinate for 3–4 hours in the refrigerator.

Preheat oven to 220°C (420°F). Heat an electric frypan or wok,
add chicken and half the marinade and stir-fry the chicken for
10 minutes or until golden.

Brush one sheet of filo pastry with butter and top with a
second sheet of pastry. Cut pastry lengthwise into 3 strips.
Spoon a portion of the filling into the corner of one end of
a pastry strip. Fold pastry diagonally over filling, from one
corner to the opposite side, to form a triangle. Continue to
fold pastry, making a triangle every time, until whole strip
is used. Brush triangle with butter on both sides and put on
a baking tray. Repeat until all filling and all pastry are used.
Bake triangles in the oven for 15 minutes, or until pastry is
golden brown and flaking.

In a saucepan, combine the ingredients for the peanut sauce and
cook for 2 minutes. Allow to cool slightly before serving.

Serve with peanut sauce, for dipping.

SAUSAGE ROLLS

1 quantity flaky pastry
500 g (1 lb) sausage meat
beaten egg, for glazing

Makes 24 small sausage rolls

Preheat oven to 220°C (420°F). Divide pastry in half. Cut each half into a 7.5 x 30 cm (3 x 12 in) strip.

Form sausage meat into 2 rolls, each 30 cm (12 in) long. Lay a sausage meat roll close to the edge of each pastry strip. Dampen one side of pastry with water, then fold pastry over and press edges together firmly.

Glaze tops of long sausage roll with beaten egg then cut each roll into 12 pieces. Place rolls on a baking tray and bake in the oven for 15 minutes. Reduce oven temperature to moderately hot (200°C/375°F) and bake for a further 10–15 minutes.

YOGURT AND CUCUMBER DIP

250 g (8 oz) plain yogurt
1 medium cucumber
1 clove garlic, crushed
1 tablespoon olive oil
1 teaspoon dill, chopped
2 teaspoons lemon juice
salt to taste
selection of crackers

Serves 6–8

Drain yogurt by placing in a muslin-lined strainer over a bowl for at
least an hour.
   Wash and grate the cucumber and drain as above.
Combine yogurt, cucumber and garlic and gradually beat in olive oil,
add remaining ingredients.
   Chill then serve with a selection of cracker biscuits.

DUCK PANCAKES

1 Chinese barbecued duck
4 shallots (scallions), cut into thin pieces 10 cm (4 in)
   long
1 Lebanese cucumber, cut into thin pieces
   10 cm (4 in) long
24 Chinese pancakes or burrito tortillas
hoisin sauce to serve

Makes 24

Remove skin and meat from duck and slice thinly. Warm pancakes
or burritos according to packet directions.

Divide duck, spring onions and cucumber evenly between
pancakes. Spoon over a little hoisin sauce and fold over pancakes.
You may need toothpicks to hold them together for serving.

Serve warm.

You can substitute Chinese pancakes for burrito tortillas and cut
them into quarters.

SHRIMP COCKTAIL

250 g (8 oz) shrimp, cooked and peeled
4 large lettuce leaves, finely shredded
slices of lemon, to garnish

COCKTAIL SAUCE
3 tablespoons thick mayonnaise
1 tablespoon tomato ketchup, or thick tomato purée,
    or skinned fresh sieved tomatoes
1 tablespoon Worcestershire sauce
2 tablespoons full cream or evaporated milk

SEASONING
pinch of celery salt or chopped celery
onion, finely chopped
lemon juice

Serves 4

To make the cocktail sauce, mix all the sauce ingredients together
in a bowl. Add seasoning and adjust if necessary.
    This dish can be arranged in glasses or small flat plates.
Place lettuce in cocktail dish and top with shrimp, cover with sauce,
and garnish with lemon slices. Serve as cold as possible.

CHICKEN NUGGETS

500 g (1 lb) chicken thigh fillets
2 tablespoons lemon juice
1 small clove garlic, crushed
salt and freshly ground black pepper
oil for deep frying
120 g (4 oz) plain flour
1 egg, beaten with a little water
1 cup dried breadcrumbs
1 teaspoon lemon pepper

Serves 6

Cut each thigh fillet into four. Place in a glass bowl and add lemon juice, garlic, salt and pepper. Cover and marinate for 30 minutes or longer.

Place the flour onto a sheet of kitchen paper, the beaten egg onto a shallow plate. Mix the breadcrumbs with the lemon pepper and place onto kitchen paper.

Coat each piece of thigh meat with the flour, dip into the egg, turn to coat then lift out with a fork, drain and toss in the breadcrumbs, ensuring the chicken is well coated.

As each piece is crumbed place in a single layer on a tray and refrigerate until time to cook. Heat oil to 180°C (350°F) in a deep fryer or saucepan. Oil must be 8 cm (3 in) deep. Fry nuggets a few at a time until golden; about 4 minutes. Drain well on absorbent paper. Serve hot with a dipping sauce.

MINI BEEF SATAYS

750 g (1 ½ lb) lean rump, boneless blade or topside
   steak
60 ml (2 fl oz) white wine
2 teaspoons soy sauce
2 teaspoons satay sauce
¼ teaspoon chilli sauce
1 clove garlic, crushed
1 tablespoon soft brown sugar

Makes 24

Soak 24 cocktail bamboo skewers for 30 minutes to prevent
burning. Slice meat thinly and evenly into 8 cm (3 in) strips.
Weave strips onto skewers.

   Combine wine, sauces, garlic and brown sugar and place in a
glass or ceramic dish. Add the satays, turning them in the mixture
to coat. Leave to marinate in the mixture for at least 30 minutes,
turning occasionally.

   Remove grill pan and heat grill on high. Place satays on cold
grill pan (to prevent them sticking during cooking) and cook under
grill for 4–5 minutes each side, basting occasionally with remaining
marinade. Garnish with chilli.

PASTA, RICE & NOODLES

COOKING PASTA

To cook pasta, bring 3.5 L (7 ½ pints) salted water to a brisk boil. Add a small amount of pasta at a time. If you are cooking spaghetti, hold it near the end and gently lower the other end into the boiling water; it gradually softens and curves around the pan as it enters the water. Boil pasta briskly, uncovered, stirring occasionally until just tender. The Italians call it 'al dente' – the pasta should be firm when bitten between the teeth. Do not overcook. Drain in a colander, rinse with hot water and stir through a dash of olive oil and salt (optional).

COOKING RICE

To boil rice to serve 4 people, pour 2 cups of rice into a large saucepan of fast-boiling, salted water and boil for 15 minutes. Rice should be just tender. Drain and serve immediately. To steam rice, wash 2 cups of long grain rice and drain well in a colander. Place rice in a saucepan with 3 cups of water and bring to the boil. Lower heat to medium and cook uncovered until water is absorbed. Remove from heat, empty rice into a colander and steam over fast boiling water for 25–30 minutes.

COOKING NOODLES

Use fresh Asian noodles direct from the packet, as they are usually already cooked and require no further preparation. If you do need to cook noodles it is a good idea to rinse them in cold water and drain them after cooking to remove the starch. Cook noodles for 2 minutes in rapidly boiling water or follow the packet instructions.

BROWN RICE WITH CHEESE

30 g (1 oz) butter
2 tablespoons oil
1½ cup shallots (scallions), chopped
500 g (1 lb) brown rice, washed and drained
1.5 L (3 pints) chicken stock, heated
1 teaspoon salt
½ teaspoon freshly ground black pepper
250 g (8 oz) Swiss cheese, sliced, or 180 g (6 oz)
   grated cheese
parsley sprigs, to garnish

Serves 6

Heat butter and oil in a large saucepan. Gently fry shallots until
soft and golden. Add rice and fry, stirring continuously, for about
8 minutes. Add stock, salt and pepper and stir through. Cover and
simmer for 1 hour. Turn into a buttered ovenproof dish.

   Cover top of rice with Swiss cheese and place under a hot grill
or in a hot oven (220°C/420°F) until cheese melts and turns golden.

   Garnish with parsley sprigs and serve hot.

CANNELLONI STUFFED WITH RICOTTA IN TOMATO SAUCE

12 cannelloni tubes
3 cups ricotta cheese
2 eggs
4 shallots (scallions), finely sliced
60 g (2 oz) Parmesan cheese
salt and freshly ground black pepper, to taste
pinch of ground nutmeg
4–6 large ripe tomatoes, skinned and chopped
3 tablespoons olive oil
60 g (2 oz) butter

Serves 4–6

Preheat oven to 180°C (350°F). Cook cannelloni according to packet instructions. Set aside until ready to fill.

In a bowl, mix ricotta cheese, eggs, spring onions and ¼ cup Parmesan cheese thoroughly. Season with salt, pepper and nutmeg.

Place tomatoes in a saucepan and cook, uncovered, until they are a thick pulp, stirring occasionally. Remove from heat and stir in oil gradually.

Drain cannelloni and fill with ricotta cheese mixture. Place filled cannelloni side by side in a single layer in a buttered shallow baking dish. Pour tomato sauce around and over the cannelloni, sprinkle with remaining Parmesan cheese and dot with butter. Bake in the oven until bubbling, about 20 minutes. Serve at once.

FETTUCCINE ALFREDO

250 g (8 oz) fettuccine
125 g (4 oz) butter
125 g (4 oz) Parmesan cheese, grated
$\frac{1}{4}$ teaspoon salt
freshly ground black pepper, to taste
250 ml (8 fl oz) fresh cream
parsley, finely chopped and extra Parmesan cheese,
   to garnish

Serves 6

Cook fettuccine for 15 minutes, or until al dente, in a large saucepan of rapidly boiling, salted water.

Meanwhile, melt butter in a large saucepan, then add Parmesan cheese, salt, pepper and cream. Cook over a low heat, stirring constantly, until blended.

Drain fettuccine. Immediately add to cheese mixture and toss until pasta is well coated. Place in a heated serving dish, sprinkle with parsley and Parmesan cheese and serve at once.

FRIED RICE

220 g (7½ oz) rice, uncooked
250 ml (8 fl oz) water, salted for boiling
2 eggs
1 teaspoon oil
250 g (½ lb) lean pork, chopped and fried quickly in oil
250 g (½ lb) shrimp, cooked and chopped
5 mushrooms, thinly sliced
4 shallots (scallions), chopped
salt, to taste
4 teaspoons soy sauce

Serves 4–6

Wash rice several times in cold water to remove excess starch.
Place rice in a saucepan of boiling, salted water and cook for
15 minutes or until grains are just tender – do not overcook.
Drain rice and allow to cool completely.

   Beat eggs lightly in a bowl, then heat oil in a frying pan and
fry as a thin pancake or omelet. Remove from pan and slice into
strips. (If you prefer, eggs can be beaten and added to the rice last,
instead of frying beforehand.)

   Place enough oil in a large pan to cover the base and heat it.
When hot, add prepared rice slowly, to avoid clumping, and stir
for about 10 minutes or until rice is thoroughly heated through.
Stir vigorously, breaking up any lumps.

   Add pork, shrimp, mushrooms, shallots and salt, then fold in egg
pieces (or beaten egg) and soy sauce. Mix well and serve.

GNOCCHI

3 medium-sized potatoes, washed
125 g (4 oz) plain (all-purpose) flour, sifted
1 egg
1½ teaspoons salt
extra flour
Italian Tomato Sauce (see page 366)
   or Bolognese Sauce (see page 356)
Parmesan cheese, grated, to garnish

Serves 4

Boil unpeeled potatoes until tender. Peel while hot and place in a mixing bowl. Mash potatoes straight away, adding sifted flour, a little at a time, while potatoes are still hot. Add egg and salt and beat until smooth.

Turn onto a well-floured board. Knead, working in enough flour to form a smooth, soft, non-sticky dough. Divide dough into several parts. Roll each to pencil thickness. Cut into 2 cm (¾ in) pieces. With the tines of a floured fork, press each piece so that it curls. Place on waxed paper. Sprinkle lightly with flour. Cook immediately, or within 2 hours.

Add gnocchi a little at a time to a large pan of rapidly boiling salted water with a little oil added. Cook for about 5 minutes, or until gnocchi comes to the surface. Drain and keep warm in a heated bowl until all gnocchi is cooked.

Serve in Tomato Sauce or Bolognese Sauce, sprinkled with Parmesan cheese.

ITALIAN MARINARA

1 kg (2 lb) marinara mix – oysters, scallops, shrimp,
   crayfish (all shelled), fish fillet pieces
60 ml (2 fl oz) olive oil
2 cloves garlic, sliced
2 x 425 g (1 lb 12 oz) tin tomatoes, puréed
1½ teaspoons salt
1 teaspoon oregano
1 teaspoon parsley, chopped
¼ teaspoon freshly ground black pepper
2 tablespoons red wine (optional)
375 g (12 oz) fettuccine or spaghetti

Serves 6–8

Wash and drain the marinara mix. Heat oil in a large frying pan
and sauté marinara mix over a medium heat for 5 minutes.
Remove from pan and keep warm. Add garlic to the pan and sauté
until golden. Stir in tomatoes, salt, oregano, parsley, pepper and
wine (if using). Cook rapidly, uncovered, for 15 minutes, or until
sauce has thickened. Stir occasionally. If sauce becomes too thick,
add ¼–½ cup water. Add marinara mix and reheat gently.

Meanwhile, cook spaghetti in boiling, salted water and drain.
Serve immediately with marinara sauce poured on top.

LASAGNE

2 tablespoons olive oil
250 g (8 oz) minced beef
250 g (8 oz) minced pork
1 onion, finely chopped
1 glove garlic, finely chopped
1 teaspoon parsley, chopped
250 g (8 oz) tomato paste
470 ml (16 fl oz) water
½ teaspoon salt
½ teaspoon freshly ground black pepper
250 g (8 oz) lasagne sheets
30 g (1 oz) mozzarella cheese, sliced thinly
250 g (8 oz) ricotta cheese, crumbed
2 tablespoons Romano cheese, grated

Serves 4–6

Heat oil in saucepan, add beef and pork and brown with onion, garlic and parsley. Stir in tomato paste, water, salt and pepper and simmer for 1½ hours.

Preheat oven to 180°C (350°F). Bring a large saucepan of water to the boil, add 1½ teaspoons salt and the lasagne sheets. Boil for 20 minutes, stirring constantly to prevent noodles sticking, until tender. Drain.

In a greased casserole dish about 5 cm (2 in) deep, arrange alternate layers of lasagne sheets, sauce, mozzarella and ricotta cheese. Repeat layers until noodles and sauce and two cheeses are all used, ending with ricotta cheese. Sprinkle with grated Romano cheese and bake in the oven for 25–30 minutes.

MUSHROOM AND ONION RISOTTO

30 g (1 oz) butter
1 small onion, chopped or sliced
1 rasher bacon, diced
12 button mushrooms, sliced
300 g (10 oz) arborio rice
375 ml (12 ½ fl oz) chicken stock, boiling
125 g (4 oz) cheese, grated
salt and freshly ground black pepper, to taste

Serves 4

Melt butter in a heavy-based saucepan, and fry onion, bacon and mushrooms, stirring once or twice, for 3–4 minutes. Stir in rice and cook for 1–2 minutes.

Pour in hot stock gradually, stirring constantly until liquid is absorbed. Continue stirring while adding stock until all liquid is absorbed each time. Cook rice for 30 minutes, or until it is tender. Add extra hot water or stock if necessary.

Stir through cheese, and season with salt and pepper. Serve immediately with fresh herbs, accompanied with tossed salad greens.

SHRIMP RISOTTO

500 g (1 lb) shrimp
4 tablespoons olive oil
2 small onions, finely chopped
1 tablespoon green peppercorns
250 g (½ lb) arborio rice
180 ml (6 fl oz) dry white wine
1 medium size onion, grated
squeeze lemon juice
chopped parsley and zest of 1 lemon, to garnish

Serves 4

Shell shrimp and make fish stock by boiling shells in about 970 ml
(2 pints) water to which a pinch of salt has been added. Strain and
reserve liquid. Chop shrimp and set aside.

Place 2 tablespoons oil in a frying pan and lightly brown onions.
Add green peppercorns and rice and cook, stirring constantly, until
rice is lightly browned. Add wine. When wine has evaporated, add
stock, gradually. Stir very lightly and simmer gently, uncovered,
until rice is cooked. Add a little hot water or more wine if rice gets
too dry.

Meanwhile, heat remaining oil in a saucepan and add grated
onion, lemon juice and chopped shrimp. Fry lightly until onion is
translucent and shrimp are cooked – approximately 3 minutes.
Stir through rice and serve sprinkled with parsley and lemon zest.

RAVIOLI

FILLING
2 tablespoons olive oil
375 g (12 ½ oz) minced beef or shredded chicken
250 g (8 oz) cooked spinach or frozen spinach, thawed
2 eggs, beaten
1 tablespoon Parmesan cheese
¾ teaspoon salt
¼ teaspoon freshly ground black pepper
500 g (1 lb) basic pasta dough
Italian tomato sauce (see page 366)
grated Parmesan or Romano cheese, to garnish

Serves 6

To make filling, heat oil in a frying pan. Add meat and cook until browned, then place meat in a bowl. Prepare and cook spinach, draining it well. Finely chop spinach and mix with meat. Add eggs, Parmesan cheese, salt and pepper. Mix well. Set aside until ready to use.

Divide pasta dough into quarters. Roll each quarter until it is 3 mm (⅛ in) thick, and a rectangular shape. Cut dough lengthways (using a pastry cutter, if you have one) into strips 12 cm (5 in) wide. Place 2 teaspoons of filling in the centre of one half of the pastry every 8.5 cm (3½ in), then fold over the other half covering the filling. Seal the whole strip by pressing the long edges together with the tines of a fork. Press the two layers of pastry together between the mounds of filling and cut in the middle between mounds with the pastry cutter, again sealing the cut edges with the tines of a fork.

Add ravioli gradually, about a third at a time, to a large saucepan of rapidly boiling, salted water. Cook for 20 minutes or until tender. Remove with a slotted spoon. Drain well.

Serve topped with heated tomato sauce and sprinkled with Parmesan cheese.

SAFFRON RISOTTO

60 g (2 oz) butter
1 large onion, finely chopped
500 g (1 lb) long grain rice, washed and drained
875 ml (1⁴/₅ pints) chicken stock
1 packet powdered saffron or a large pinch of saffron
   strands
2 teaspoons salt
10 whole black peppercorns

Serves 6–8

Heat butter in a saucepan and gently fry onion for 5 minutes or until golden. Add rice and fry for 2–3 minutes, until all rice grains are coated with butter.

In a saucepan, heat chicken stock. Add hot stock, saffron, salt and peppercorns to the rice. Bring to the boil, then reduce heat, cover tightly and steam for 20 minutes. Remove cover and fluff up rice gently with a fork.

Serve as an accompaniment to fish, poultry or any kind of meat.

SEAFOOD RISOTTO

125 ml (4 fl oz) olive oil
2 cloves garlic, chopped
1 medium onion, chopped
660 g (1½ lbs) arborio rice
1 bunch shallots (scallions), chopped
1 bunch fresh coriander (cilantro), chopped
4 pieces butternut pumpkin, cooked
1 L (2 pints) fish stock
250 ml (8 fl oz) white wine
1 kg (2 lb) marinara mix
¾ cup Parmesan cheese, grated
salt and freshly ground black pepper, to taste
3 tablespoons sour cream

Serves 6

Heat oil in a large saucepan and gently fry onion and garlic.
When onion is translucent, add rice. Stir well, until rice is coated
with oil. Add shallots and coriander and cook for a few minutes,
then add pumpkin.

Add 250 ml (1 cup) stock, stirring constantly until it is absorbed.
Add 250 ml (1 cup) wine and continue to stir. Continue to add stock
by the cup (and stir regularly), until all stock is absorbed. It will take
about 30 minutes to get the rice to an almost cooked stage.

When rice is almost cooked, fold in the marinara mix and cook
for a further 5 minutes. Add Parmesan. Season with salt and
pepper. Cook for another few minutes, until seafood is done, then
stir in sour cream.

Serve in bowls, and sprinkle the last of the Parmesan on top.

SPAGHETTI BOLOGNESE

1 tablespoon olive oil
250 g (½ lb) minced beef
1 clove garlic, crushed
1 large onion (or 2 small onions), finely grated
500 g (1 lb) peeled tomatoes, chopped
1 teaspoon oregano or basil
1 teaspoon salt
freshly ground black pepper, to taste
1 teaspoon sugar
3 tablespoons tomato paste
250 ml (8 fl oz) beef stock (see page 376)
250 g (½ lb) spaghetti
Parmesan cheese, to garnish

Serves 4

Heat oil in frying pan, add meat, garlic and onion and brown lightly.
Add tomatoes, oregano, salt, pepper and sugar. In a small bowl,
blend tomato paste with stock. Add this to mixture in frying pan.
Simmer for 30 minutes, uncovered, so that sauce thickens slightly.

When sauce is almost ready, cook spaghetti in boiling salted
water until tender. Drain spaghetti, and place on a hot serving dish
or plate. Pour hot sauce over spaghetti and sprinkle with Parmesan
cheese. Serve additional cheese in a small bowl.

SPAGHETTI CARBONARA

250–375 g (8–12 oz) fettuccine
2 tablespoons olive oil
3 slices bacon, finely diced
2 eggs
45 g (1½ oz) Parmesan cheese, grated
250 ml (8 fl oz) fresh cream
freshly ground black pepper, to taste

Serves 4

Add fettuccine into boiling, salted water and cook for 8 minutes or until al dente.

Just before fettuccine is ready, heat oil and fry bacon.

In a bowl, beat in eggs and add cheese.

Drain pasta and return to the hot saucepan. Add cheese mixture, cream, plenty of black pepper and crisp bacon. Mix well. Place the saucepan over a low heat for a minute or so, stirring constantly.

Place in a hot dish and serve immediately.

SPAGHETTI WITH MEATBALLS

TOMATO SAUCE
1 x 500 g (1 lb) can
   whole tomatoes
250 ml (8 fl oz) Italian
   tomato sauce
   (see page 366)
125 g (4 oz)
   tomato paste
60 ml (2 fl oz) water
60 ml (2 fl oz) red
   wine (or water)
2 bay leaves, crushed
2 tablespoons parsley,
   chopped
1 clove garlic, crushed

MEATBALLS
4 slices white bread
500 g (1 lb) minced chuck
   or round steak
1 tablespoon Parmesan
   cheese, grated
1 tablespoon parsley, chopped
1 tablespoon onion, grated
2 teaspoons salt
¼ teaspoon black pepper
¼ teaspoon oregano
1 egg
3 tablespoons olive oil
250 g (8 oz) spaghetti
   or thin spaghetti
Parmesan cheese

Serves 4–6

To make tomato sauce, combine all ingredients in a large saucepan. Simmer until thick, stirring occasionally for about 10 minutes.

To make meatballs, place bread in a small bowl, add enough water to cover, and let stand for 2 minutes. Remove bread and squeeze out excess water. In a larger bowl, combine bread with minced steak, Parmesan cheese, parsley, onion, salt, pepper, oregano and egg. Mix lightly until thoroughly combined. Shape into small balls. Heat oil in a frying pan and brown meatballs on all sides.

Add meatballs to sauce and simmer for 15–20 minutes. Meanwhile, cook spaghetti in salted, boiling water (about 20 minutes). Drain spaghetti and place on a hot serving dish or plate. Top with meatballs and sauce and sprinkle with Parmesan cheese.

SPAGHETTI SPRINGTIME

250 g (8 oz) cooked hot spaghetti, drained
4–6 tomatoes, skinned and chopped
1 green capsicum (bell pepper), chopped
½ cup shallots (scallions), chopped
¼ cup black olives, chopped
salt and freshly ground black pepper, to taste
juice of half a lemon
80 ml (3 fl oz) olive oil
chopped parsley, to garnish
Parmesan cheese (optional)

Serves 6–8

Put tomatoes into a saucepan and heat, stirring. When they are hot, add spaghetti, capsicum, spring onions, olives, salt and pepper, lemon juice, and enough olive oil to coat pasta. Toss well.

Sprinkle with parsley and Parmesan cheese (if using) and serve immediately.

TUNA AND RICE BAKE

RICE CRUST
750 ml (1½ pints) water
1¼ cups uncooked brown rice, well washed and
    drained
⅓ cup shallots (scallions), chopped
1 egg, lightly beaten
1 teaspoon curry powder
1½ tablespoons butter, melted

FILLING
1 x 425 g (13½ oz) can tuna in brine, drained (reserve
    liquid)
1 carrot, grated
1 zucchini (courgette), grated
60 g (2 oz) butter
30 g (1 oz) cup flour
1 teaspoon mustard powder
1 teaspoon paprika, plus extra to garnish
½ teaspoon freshly ground black pepper
375 ml (12½ fl oz) milk
2 tablespoons parsley, chopped
2 teaspoons lemon juice
60 g (2 oz) tasty cheese, grated
thin lemon slices and chopped parsley, to garnish

Serves 8

In a large saucepan, bring water to the boil. Slowly add rice. Stir once with a fork, then cover tightly with a lid. Simmer gently until all liquid is absorbed (45–50 minutes).

Preheat oven to 200°C (375°F). In a bowl, combine cooked rice with shallots, egg, curry powder and butter. Press onto base and sides of a 23 cm (9 in) square ovenproof dish.

Spread tuna evenly over rice base. Top with carrot and zucchini and set aside.

Melt butter in a saucepan, then add flour, mustard, paprika and pepper and cook for 1 minute, mixing well. Gradually blend in milk and reserved tuna liquid, and bring mixture to the boil. Then add parsley and lemon juice, and stir until smooth.

Pour sauce over vegetables, and sprinkle over cheese and paprika. Bake in the oven for 30 minutes until heated through. Serve garnished with lemon slices and chopped parsley.

FISH & SEAFOOD

COOKING FISH

For maximum freshness and flavor, buy your fresh fish on the day you intend eating it – don't store it in the refrigerator for a long time. If fish isn't prepared on the day, you can freeze it. As a general guide, allow 500 g (1 lb) of fish for each person if it includes the head and bones. When fish is filleted or cut into steaks, allow 125–250 g (4–8 oz) per person, depending on the recipe being prepared and the accompaniments being served.

Most fish shops will fillet the whole fish you buy, but if you prefer to fillet your own, here's an easy way to do it. Make a cut at the back of the head with a sharp, thin-bladed knife. Keeping close to the backbone, cut right down the tail and gently lift the fillet from the backbone using a slicing motion. Remove fins with scissors. Turn fish and repeat the process. Remove excess bones from fillets with knife or tweezers.

Whichever way you plan to cook your fish, there is usually no lengthy cooking time involved. The moment the flesh is white, moist, and flakes easily when tested with a fork, the fish is ready to eat.

GRILLING

One of the easiest ways of cooking fish is grilling – it is also a healthy method of cooking fish. Small whole fish, or steaks and fillets of larger fish and shellfish can all be grilled. Preheat the griller to a moderate heat and place the fish on the grill tray to cook. Alternatively, line a grill pan with aluminum foil and cook your fish on the stove top, regularly basting the fish while cooking (combined melted butter and lemon juice is tasty). Herbs, finely chopped onion, white wine or other seasonings of your choice may also be added to the basting sauce. The fish will be cooked in approximately 10 minutes, depending on its size and thickness. Turn the fish once only while cooking as it breaks easily – constant turning is not necessary.

FRYING

Fish may be shallow or deep fried. Deep-frying is ideal for smaller fillets of fish, or shellfish coated with batter. Shallow frying is used for fish fillets or steaks and small whole fish. Always dry pieces of fish well with absorbent paper before cooking. Most fish is coated before frying to protect the delicate flesh and keep it moist. Seasoned flour and egg and breadcrumbs are two ways of coating fish. Use peanut or avocado oil for deep-frying. For shallow frying, olive oil or butter or a combination of the two may be used.

Make sure the oil is very hot before adding prepared fish. Cook the fish quickly and when golden brown on both sides, remove the fish with a metal spatula or slotted spoon and drain on absorbent paper. Serve immediately while the fish is moist inside and the coating is crisp.

Coatings for fried fish

1   Plain (all-purpose) flour seasoned with pepper. (Salt is best added after the fish is fried.) Dry fish well and coat lightly with flour, shaking off any surplus. Small fish may be coated easily by shaking them gently in a plastic bag containing a little flour.

2   Egg and breadcrumbs. A deliciously crisp coating for fish. Dip pieces of fish in slightly beaten egg which has been diluted with a spoonful of water or oil. Coat with fine dry breadcrumbs (or crushed breakfast cereal for a different flavor) pressing the crumbs on firmly. Stand fish for at least 15 minutes before frying (the crumbs will then stay on when frying).

3   Add freshly ground black pepper, paprika, finely chopped herbs, grated Parmesan cheese or other seasonings to crumbs before coating fish, but again it is best to add salt after frying.

4   Batter is a delicious way of coating fish providing the mixture is thin and light and the cooked fish is eaten immediately while moist inside and the batter is golden brown and crisp (use batter recipe on page 119).

POACHING

This is cooking fish in a gentle simmering liquid. This method is ideal for whole fish like salmon and trout, or smoked fish. A fish kettle is ideal for poaching fish. It has an inner perforated tray to place the fish on, and when cooked, the tray can be lifted out without breaking the fish. If a fish kettle is not available, poach fish in an ordinary saucepan, but wrap it in a piece of muslin first so that it will not break up while cooking and it can be lifted out of the liquid easily. Salt water, fish stock or milk may be used as a poaching liquid. The fish should be completely covered with liquid while cooking.

Bring the liquid to the boil and immerse the fish. Return the liquid to the boil, then immediately lower the heat until the liquid is just simmering gently. Allow 6–10 minutes per 500 g (1 lb) of flesh. Remove fish from the pan immediately when the fish is cooked – overcooking means soft fish with little texture or flavor.

STEAMING

An ideal method of cooking delicately flavored fish or for those wanting an easily digestible food. Fish may be steamed in the upper half of a double boiler (the upper section having a perforated base), over gently simmering water. The fish may be wrapped in aluminum foil to protect the flesh and keep it moist.

Fillets of fish may also be steamed on a greased plate over a saucepan of gently simmering water. Season with pepper and dot with butter if desired. Cover with a second plate. Cooking should take approximately 10 minutes, depending on size of fillets.

BAKING

Fish may be baked in the oven either whole or filleted. Most fish are best baked whole, as the outer skin protects the flesh and keeps it moist. There are many delicious stuffings for whole fish baked in the oven. Bake in a hot oven 200–230°C (400–450°F). The length of time will depend on the size of the fish. Either bake in a baking dish and baste with butter and lemon juice while cooking or wrap in aluminum foil, placing small pieces of butter over the fish and a little lemon juice or white wine. Fish is cooked when flesh flakes easily with a fork (test the thickest part of the fish).

Small fillets can be baked in a very hot oven 230–260°C (450–550°F). They may be coated with seasoned breadcrumbs, grated cheese, and sliced tomatoes. But if preferred, dot with butter, add a little lemon juice and baste regularly while cooking. The fish will take approximately 10 minutes to cook. The liquid that drains away from the fish while baking should be used in any sauce being made to serve with the fish.

BARBECUING

Whole fish, fish steaks, fillets of fish and shellfish can all be barbecued. Whole fish may be barbecued in wire frames, turning frequently. No basting is required, but when cooked and ready to serve, brush the fish with butter and lemon juice and season with salt and pepper. Small fish, freshly caught, may be threaded on stainless steel skewers for barbecuing or they may be cooked in wire frames placed flat over the fire.

Fish steaks, fillets of fish and shellfish may be barbecued directly over glowing coals or cooked in a cast iron skillet or on a hotplate.

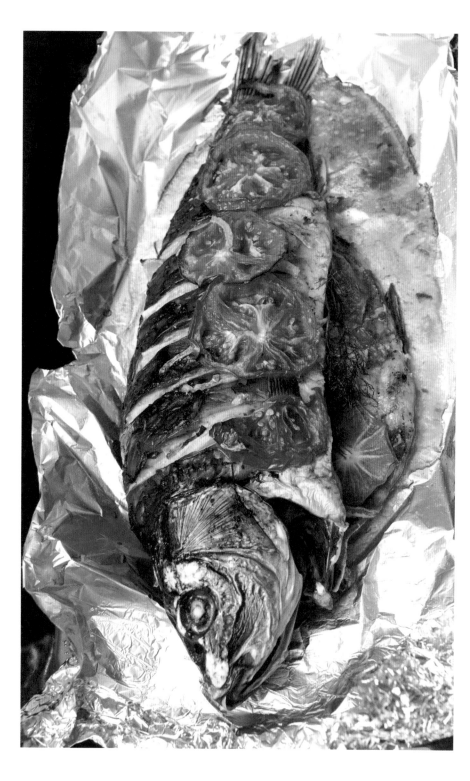

BAKED FISH

1 large snapper, mullet or redfish, cleaned
1 teaspoon salt
¼ teaspoon white pepper
2 onions, sliced
4 ripe tomatoes, skinned and thickly sliced
½ teaspoon ground allspice
¼ teaspoon extra salt
¼ teaspoon black peppercorns, crushed
½ teaspoon cayenne pepper
2 tablespoons brown sugar
125 ml (4 fl oz) vinegar
60 ml (2 fl oz) water
60 g (2 oz) butter

Serves 4–6

Preheat oven to 150°C (300°F). Place fish in a greased baking dish and season with salt and pepper. Cover with onion and tomato. Sprinkle with allspice, extra salt, peppercorns, cayenne pepper and brown sugar. Add vinegar and water and dot with small pieces of butter. Wrap in foil.

Bake fish in the oven for 20–30 minutes, depending on the size of fish. Baste frequently. Serve with a green salad or vegetable.

DEEP-FRIED FISH

Use fillets of fish and cover with a suitable coating before frying.

For coating, use one of the following:
- seasoned flour, for sardines and anchovies
- milk and seasoned flour, for fish fillets
- seasoned flour, beaten egg and breadcrumbs, for shrimp
- batter, for fish fillets

To make seasoned flour:
add a pinch of salt and pepper to plain (all-purpose) flour. You can also add mixed herbs for a more intense flavor.

To deep-fry fish, heat enough oil to cover fish in a deep-frying pan or electric fryer. Test temperature by putting in a 2.5 cm (1 in) cube of bread – it should brown in 1 minute when the oil is at the correct temperature. Place coated fish in oil, avoiding contact between pieces. Cook for 2–3 minutes. Drain well on absorbent paper.

Serve piping hot with lemon wedges, potato fries and tartar sauce.

CRAYFISH MORNAY

1 x 1 kg (2 lb) crayfish
1 shallot (scallion), finely chopped
salt and freshly ground black pepper, to taste
cayenne pepper, to taste
paprika, to taste
30 g (1 oz) butter
150 ml (5 fl oz) mornay sauce, heated
parsley sprigs, to garnish

MORNAY SAUCE
15 g (½ oz) butter
1 tablespoon plain (all-purpose) flour
150 ml (5 fl oz) milk
60 g (2 oz) Gruyère cheese, grated
salt and freshly ground black pepper, to taste
1–2 tablespoons fresh cream

Serves 2

Wash crayfish well under warm water, then remove its head and cut the shell in half, removing the intestines at the same time. Scoop meat from shell and cut into 2 cm (1 in) cubes. Place shell halves in a hot oven (220°C/420°F) until bright red in color.

Place crayfish meat into a bowl, and add shallot, salt and pepper, and a dash of cayenne pepper. Place mixture in hot shells, sprinkle with paprika, dot with butter and place under a hot grill until the meat becomes clear white and loses its transparent appearance. Coat with mornay sauce, and replace under hot grill briefly, until golden brown – overcooking will toughen the crayfish.

Serve garnished with parsley sprigs and accompanied by thinly sliced fried potatoes and sautéed mushrooms.

FRIED LOBSTER WITH BUTTER

1 medium-sized rock lobster
½ teaspoon salt
1 teaspoon plain flour
olive oil, for frying
juice from half a lemon
lemon wedges and finely chopped parsley, to garnish

Serves 2

Cut lobster in half lengthways, then remove the bag in the head and intestine.

Sprinkle lobster meat with salt and flour. Heat olive oil in a pan and add lobster, cut side down. Fry for 15 minutes, then turn and fry for another 15 minutes. Place lobster on plate and squeeze over lemon juice.

Garnish with lemon wedges and serve with tossed salad greens.

SNAPPER FILLETS WITH WHITE WINE AND PARSLEY

60 g (2 oz) plain flour
1 teaspoon coarse ground pepper
¼ teaspoon sea salt
4 snapper fillets, about 220 g (8 oz) each
2 tablespoons olive oil
60 g (2 oz) butter
2 cloves garlic, crushed
125 ml (4 fl oz) white wine
¼ cup parsley, finely chopped

Serves 4

Combine the flour, pepper and salt in a dish and coat the fish fillets evenly, shaking off any excess.

Heat the oil in a pan, add the fish, and cook over a medium heat for 5–6 minutes on each side, depending on thickness of fish. Set fish aside on a plate, and keep warm.

Wipe out the pan, then melt butter, add garlic, and cook for 2 minutes. Add the white wine and simmer until the sauce reduces.

Just before serving, add chopped parsley to the sauce and serve with the fish.

FRIED WHITING

2–3 tablespoons lemon juice
1 onion, sliced
1 bouquet garni
500 g (1 lb) fresh whiting fillets
3 egg yolks, beaten
1 teaspoon water
3 tablespoons Parmesan cheese, finely grated
butter, for frying
lemon wedges, for serving

Serves 4–6

Combine lemon juice, onion and bouquet garni and pour over fish. Let fish and liquid stand for 1 hour; turn fish once or twice during the hour.

In a bowl, whisk together egg yolks and water. Put Parmesan cheese into another bowl, or onto a flat board, or into a clean plastic bag. Dip each piece of fish in the egg mixture, then cover it with grated cheese.

Heat butter and fry fish for approximately 20 minutes, turning once while cooking, or until cooked through and golden brown.

Serve with potato wedges and a salad.

FRIED WHITEBAIT

500 g (1 lb) fresh whitebait
plain (all-purpose) flour, for coating
olive oil for frying
rock salt, crushed
sliced lemon and fresh bread and butter, for serving

Serves 4

Rinse whitebait and drain well, then dry with absorbent paper.
Toss lightly in flour and place in a wire basket. Fry in deep, hot oil.
Drain well.

Reheat oil and fry whitebait again, until very crisp. Drain on
absorbent paper again, then sprinkle with rock salt and serve with
lemon and bread and butter.

FISH TACOS

1 egg
100 g (3⅓ oz) plain flour
½ teaspoon salt
1 teaspoon pepper
4 fillets of any firm flesh fish (such as snapper)
3 tablespoons olive oil
1 tablespoon butter
6 soft tacos, 15cm (6 in)
sweet coleslaw
coriander leaves, to garnish

Serves 4

Whisk the egg. Combine the flour, salt and pepper.

Dip the fish fillets in the egg wash, then coat the fillets in the flour mix. Place the fish fillets on a medium-high heat either on a barbecue flatplate with the oil and butter or frypan. Cook for 3-4 minutes on each side, or until golden brown.

Cut the fillets into long strips and place on the tacos with the sweet coleslaw. Garnish with coriander.

LOBSTER THERMIDOR

90 g (3 oz) butter
30 g (1 oz) plain (all-purpose) flour
270 ml (½ pint) milk
2 tablespoons thickened cream
Dijon mustard
salt and black pepper, to taste
2 medium-sized lobsters, meat removed from shells
    and diced
1 small onion or eschalot, finely chopped
2 tablespoons white wine or sherry
60 g (2 oz) Parmesan cheese, grated

Serves 4

In a saucepan, melt 30 g (1 oz) butter. Add the flour, mix well and
cook for 1–2 minutes. Stir in milk, cream, a little mustard and salt
and pepper. Add the lobster meat and heat gently.

In another pan, melt the remaining butter and fry the onion or
shallot. Add to lobster mixture, together with wine. Pile mixture into
lobster shells, cover tops with grated Parmesan cheese and brown
under a hot grill.

OYSTERS MICHELENE

12 oysters
120 g (4 oz) shrimp, peeled and deveined
30 g (1 oz) butter
cayenne pepper, to taste

Serves 1–2

Preheat oven to 220°C (420°F). Remove oysters from shells and set shells aside. Mix oysters with shrimp and chop finely. Mix with butter and cayenne pepper. Place mixture in oyster shells and cook in the oven for 3 minutes. Serve immediately.

OYSTERS MORNAY

12 large, flat oysters
salt and pepper, to taste
1 tablespoon Parmesan cheese, grated

MORNAY SAUCE
15 g (½ oz) butter
1 tablespoon plain (all-purpose) flour
150 ml (5 fl oz) milk
60 g (2 oz) Gruyère cheese, grated
salt and freshly ground black pepper, to taste
1–2 tablespoons fresh cream

Serves 1–2

Sprinkle oysters with salt and pepper and place under a hot grill
for 1 minute. Spread each oyster with mornay sauce to cover.
Sprinkle with Parmesan cheese and bake in a hot oven for
5–10 minutes or until golden brown. Serve immediately.

To make Mornay Sauce, melt butter in a small saucepan.
Blend in flour until smooth, then cook for 1–2 minutes. Add milk
and bring to the boil, stirring continuously. Remove pan from
heat and add cheese. Stir until cheese melts. Season with salt
and pepper and add enough cream to make the sauce a good
coating consistency.

OYSTERS NATURAL

12 oysters
lemon wedges

COCKTAIL SAUCE
2 tablespoons tomato ketchup
1 teaspoon Worcestershire sauce
2 teaspoons cream
pinch of ground black pepper

Serves 1–2

Arrange oysters on a bed of crushed ice with lemon wedges.
Serve with chilled cocktail sauce in a small bowl in the centre of
the plate.

To make Cocktail Sauce, combine all ingredients together until
well blended.

TUNA MORNAY

500 g (1 lb) potatoes, boiled
30 g (1 oz) margarine
2 tablespoons milk
salt and pepper, to taste
300 g (10½ oz) can tuna in brine
315 ml (10½ fl oz) béchamel sauce (see page 354)
30–60 g (2–3 oz) tasty cheese, grated

Serves 4

Preheat oven to 180°C (350°F). Mash the potatoes and beat in the margarine, milk and salt and pepper. Line the sides and bottom of a shallow ovenproof dish with mashed potato, then put flaked tuna on top of potato on the bottom of the dish. Make (or heat, if it's already made) béchamel sauce, stir in cheese, then spoon sauce over tuna.

Bake in a moderate oven for 15 minutes or until fish is golden on top.

POACHED FISH IN WHITE WINE SAUCE

750 g–1 kg (1½–2 lb) fish fillets (bream or sole)
375 ml (12½ fl oz) court bouillon
375 ml (12½ fl oz) dry white wine
pinch of tarragon
1 small onion, finely chopped
3 egg yolks
3 tablespoons fresh cream
salt and pepper, to taste

Serves 4

Prepare fish and poach in court bouillon. Drain well and keep hot. Place wine, tarragon and onion in a saucepan and bring to the boil. Add court bouillon and boil continuously, until volume is reduced by half. Allow to cool.

In a bowl, beat egg yolks with cream. Add to cooled liquid and reheat gently, without boiling. Season with salt and pepper, pour over the poached fish fillets, and serve.

SEAFOOD CHOWDER

500 g (1 lb) marinara mix – fish pieces, shelled
  shrimps, oysters, scallops, crab
750 ml (1½ pints) water
30 g (1 oz) butter
1 onion, sliced
1 potato, sliced
½ teaspoon saffron (optional)
salt, to taste
250 ml (8 fl oz) milk
60–125 ml (2–4 fl oz) fresh cream
salt and freshly ground black pepper, to taste
1 tablespoon parsley, finely chopped to garnish

Serves 4–6

Poach seafood in salted water until just tender. Strain stock,
taking care to remove any skin or bones from fish and set aside.
Reserve seafood for later.

Melt butter in a saucepan and sauté onion and potato for
2 minutes. Add strained stock, saffron and salt. Simmer for
20 minutes, then purée in a blender or food processor until smooth.

Return soup to saucepan, add milk and bring to the boil.
Add cream and seafood and season to taste. Heat gently but do
not boil.

Sprinkle with parsley and serve with crusty bread.

SEAFOOD PAELLA

60 ml (2 fl oz) olive oil
2 tablespoons butter
2 cloves garlic, chopped
1 onion, chopped
1 capsicum (bell pepper), seeded and chopped
3 tomatoes, peeled
330 g (10½ oz) short grain rice
825 ml (1¾ pints) fish stock
1 teaspoon salt
¼ teaspoon saffron threads, crumbled
mixture of seafood – shrimp, peeled and deveined,
    scallops, mussels, uncooked crab
¼ teaspoon freshly ground black pepper
3 tablespoons fresh parsley, chopped
2 teaspoons fresh oregano, chopped
1 teaspoon fresh thyme, chopped

Serves 8

In a large frying pan (that has a lid), heat oil and butter over a
medium heat. Add garlic, onion and capsicum, and cook until tender
(about 10 minutes). Stir in tomatoes and cook for about 5 minutes.
Add rice and stir. Then stir in fish stock, salt and saffron. Cover and
bring to boil, then remove lid, reduce heat and simmer for
5 minutes, stirring continually.

Add seafood, then cover and simmer for a further 5 minutes.
Add pepper, parsley, oregano, thyme and cook, still covered, until
tender (about 10–15 minutes).

POULTRY

CHICKEN KIEV MACADAMIA

6 large single chicken breasts, boned
salt and freshly ground black pepper, to taste
180 g (6 oz) chilled butter, cut into 6 even chunks
3 cloves garlic, halved then crushed
3 teaspoons parsley, chopped
125 g (4 oz) plain (all-purpose) flour,
    seasoned with salt and black pepper
2 eggs, beaten
¼ cup ground macadamia nuts
oil, for frying

Serves 6

Pound chicken breasts flat with a meat tenderizer. Sprinkle breasts
on both sides with salt and pepper and lay them skin side down.
In the centre of each breast put 1 chunk of chilled butter, ½ clove
crushed garlic and ½ teaspoon chopped parsley. Roll each breast in
towards the centre, then tie each one securely with string.

Roll breasts in seasoned flour, dip in egg and then roll in ground
macadamia nuts. Press nuts on firmly and chill breasts for at least
30 minutes.

Deep-fry breasts in hot oil (190°C/375°F) for 5 minutes.
Lift them out and gently remove the string. Return breasts to oil for
10–12 minutes, or until cooked. Drain breasts on absorbent paper
and serve immediately.

CHICKEN SUPREME

1 x 1.5 kg (3 lb) chicken, cooked and boned
1 large green capsicum (bell pepper),
   seeds and pith removed and sliced
60 g (2 oz) button mushrooms,
   washed and cut into quarters
45 g (1½ oz) butter
2 tablespoons plain (all-purpose) flour
315 ml (10½ fl oz) chicken stock
3 tablespoons fresh cream
½ teaspoon salt
freshly ground black pepper, to taste

Serves 4

Preheat oven to 180°C (350°F). Cut chicken meat into bite-sized pieces.

Blanch capsicum in boiling salted water for 2–3 minutes, then drain. Melt 15 g (½ oz) butter in a frying pan and sauté capsicum and mushrooms for 2–3 minutes. Set aside.

Melt remaining butter in a flameproof casserole dish (use one that has a lid). Add flour and blend until smooth, then cook for 10 minutes until golden. Add stock and bring to the boil, stirring continuously. Add cream and boil rapidly until sauce has a syrupy consistency. Add seasonings, chicken, capsicum and mushrooms. Mix thoroughly, then cover and cook in the oven for 20 minutes, or until hot.

Served on a bed of steamed rice.

CHICKEN FINGERS

1 kg (2 lbs) chicken tenderloins
1 clove garlic, crushed
2 tablespoons lemon juice
½ teaspoon salt
¼ teaspoon pepper
120 g (4 oz) plain (all-purpose) flour
2 eggs, beaten with 1 tablespoon water
140 g (5 oz) dried breadcrumbs
125 ml (4 fl oz) canola oil

DIPPING SAUCE
125 ml (4 fl oz) sweet chili sauce
1 teaspoon soy sauce
1 tablespoon honey

Serves 4

Place tenderloins in a large non-metallic dish. Add garlic, lemon juice, salt and pepper and marinate for one hour. Remove from marinade and coat with flour. Dip into the egg then cover with breadcrumbs, making sure to press crumbs on firmly. Place in a single layer on a flat tray. Refrigerate until ready for use.

Add enough oil to cover the base of a large frying pan and heat. Test with a piece of chicken – if it sizzles, the oil is ready. Add one layer of tenderloins and fry about two minutes each side until golden. Remove and drain on absorbent paper. Add more oil if necessary and cook the remainder. Place chicken on a large platter.

To make dipping sauce, combine the sweet chili sauce, soy sauce and honey together. Serve chicken with dipping sauce on the side.

CASHEW NUT BUTTER CHICKEN

500 g (1 lb) skinless chicken thigh fillets
50 g (1¾ oz) ghee (clarified butter)
2 cloves garlic, crushed
2 onions, minced
1 tablespoon Madras curry paste
1 tablespoon ground coriander (cilantro)
½ teaspoon ground nutmeg
50 g (1¾ oz) cashew nuts, roasted and ground
315 ml (10½ fl oz) double cream
2 tablespoons coconut milk

Serves 4

Cut chicken into 2 cm (¾ in) cubes. Melt ghee in a saucepan over medium heat, add garlic and onion and cook, stirring, for 3 minutes or until onion turns golden.

Stir in curry paste, coriander and nutmeg and cook for 2 minutes or until fragrant. Add chicken and cook, stirring, for 5 minutes or until chicken is brown.

Add cashews, cream and coconut milk and simmer, stirring occasionally, for 40 minutes or until chicken is tender. To roast cashews, spread nuts over a baking tray and bake at 180°C (360°F) for 5–10 minutes or until lightly and evenly browned. Toss back and forth occasionally with a spoon to ensure even browning. Alternatively, place nuts under a medium grill and cook, tossing back and forth until roasted.

CHICKEN TERIYAKI

2 tablespoons butter
80 ml (3 fl oz) teriyaki sauce or soy sauce
2.5 cm (1 in) piece ginger, chopped
2 tablespoons sugar
2 tablespoons dry sherry
500 g (1 lb/2 large) boneless chicken breasts, skinned
8 shallots (scallions), cut into 2.5 cm (1 in) strips
bamboo skewers, soaked in water

Serves 4

Place butter, teriyaki sauce, ginger, sugar and dry sherry in a small pan and stir over a medium heat until sugar is dissolved. Cool.

Cut chicken into 2.5 cm (1 in) pieces and stir into marinade with shallots. Chill for at least 2 hours.

Thread chicken and shallots onto bamboo skewers and grill for 4–5 minutes on either side, or until cooked, brushing occasionally with marinade.

Serve with steamed rice and salad.

CURRIED CHICKEN

1 x 1.5 kg (3 lb) chicken, cut into chunks
60 g (2 oz) butter
2 onions, chopped
1 tablespoon curry powder
1 teaspoon curry paste
1 tablespoon plain (all-purpose) flour
500 ml (1 pint) chicken stock
1 clove garlic, crushed
salt and freshly ground black pepper, to taste
1 tablespoon redcurrant jelly
125 ml (4 fl oz) coconut milk
60 ml (2 fl oz) fresh cream

Serves 6

Preheat oven to 180°C (350°F). Melt butter in a flameproof
casserole dish (use one that has a lid) and fry chicken until
golden brown. Remove chicken and sauté onion in remaining
butter until golden. Add curry powder and paste and continue
to cook for 3–4 minutes. Add flour and blend until smooth.
Stirring continuously, add stock and bring to the boil.
Replace chicken in casserole, add garlic and season with salt
and pepper.

Cover casserole dish and cook in the oven for 45 minutes, or
until chicken is tender. Place chicken on a serving dish and keep
warm. Add redcurrant jelly and coconut milk to curry sauce, bring
to the boil and simmer for 5 minutes. Add cream and spoon sauce
over chicken pieces.

Serve with boiled rice and chutney.

EASY CURRIED CHICKEN

60 g (2 oz) butter
1 kg (2 lb) chicken breast, sliced into 2 cm strips
2 teaspoons curry powder
1 onion, diced
2 rashers bacon, diced
2 carrots, sliced
1 stick celery, sliced
1 cup peas, cooked
470 g (15 oz) can tomatoes
1 tablespoon pickles, diced
1 teaspoon tomato sauce
1 teaspoon Worcestershire sauce

Serves 6

Melt half the butter in a frying pan and quickly fry the chicken strips. The chicken should be colored on the outside, and still pink in the middle. Set aside.

Melt remaining butter in a frying pan and add curry powder (use more than suggested if you like your curries hot). Add onion and bacon and fry for 5 minutes or until soft. Add remaining ingredients. If the dish seems to be too dry, add 180 ml (6 fl oz) water with 2 beef stock cubes dissolved in it. Lastly add the chicken and simmer for 1 hour.

Serve with boiled or steamed rice and condiments such as desiccated coconut, cucumber sliced into yogurt and fruit chutney.

THAI CHICKEN CURRY

1 tablespoon canola oil
4 chicken thigh fillets, finely sliced
3 tablespoons yellow curry paste
1 onion, finely chopped
2 cm (around ¾oz) piece of ginger, grated
1 clove garlic, finely chopped
1 eggplant (aubergine), roughly chopped
500 ml (1 pint) coconut cream
½ cup frozen peas
2 tablespoons oyster sauce
1 teaspoon fish sauce
½ cup cashews
chillies sliced (optional) add more for heat
½ cup fresh coriander (cilantro)
rice, to serve

Serves 4

Heat oil in a wok or large frying pan, add chicken and cook for
1–2 minutes. Remove and set aside.

Add curry paste, fry for 1 minute or until fragrant, then add
onion, ginger, garlic and aubergine. Stir-fry for 1–2 minutes.
Return chicken to the wok, add coconut cream and simmer for
10 minutes. Add peas, oyster sauce and fish sauce. Cook for a
further 2 minutes.

Serve the curry with rice, garnished with the cashews
and coriander.

GARLIC AND HERB CHICKEN

90 g (3 oz) butter, softened
1 garlic clove, crushed
2 tablespoons shallots (scallions), chopped
2 tablespoons parsley, chopped
2 teaspoons prepared mustard
4 chicken Maryland pieces
pinch of paprika
baking paper
aluminum foil

Serves 4

Preheat oven to 200°C (400°F).

In a bowl, combine butter with garlic, shallots, parsley and mustard, and mix well. Carefully lift skin from flesh of chicken, and spread flavored butter over flesh. Dust chicken pieces with paprika, then wrap chicken individually in baking paper, and then in foil.

Bake in the oven for 20 minutes, then open foil and baking paper and cook for a further 20 minutes.

Serve with tossed salad.

SAUTÉED CHICKEN

1 x 2 kg (4 lb) chicken
flour, to coat
90 g (3 oz) butter
salt and freshly ground black pepper, to taste
250 ml (½ pint) dry white wine
chopped parsley or chives, to garnish

Serves 4

Cut chicken into 4 joints and dip in flour. Heat butter in a large, heavy, deep-frying pan and brown chicken pieces, turning each piece so that it colors evenly. When browned, add salt and pepper and wine. Reduce heat, cover and continue cooking for 30 minutes or until chicken is tender.

Turn chicken pieces two or three times during cooking to absorb the flavors.

When chicken is cooked, remove and keep warm. Add a little more wine if the pan is quite dry, and let pan juices cook over increased heat for a few minutes.

Pour sauce over chicken, garnish with chopped parsley or chives and serve.

ROAST CHICKEN

1 x 1.5 kg (3 lb) chicken, washed and dried
salt and freshly ground black pepper, to taste
3 tablespoons olive oil
315 ml (10½ fl oz) chicken stock

Serves 6

Preheat oven to 180°C (350°F).
   Rub chicken with salt, pepper and half the olive oil.
Truss chicken and place in a greased roasting pan with remaining
oil. Cook in the oven, basting occasionally, for 1 hour, or until
tender and golden brown all over. Remove chicken and keep warm.
While chicken is cooking make chicken stock.
   Add chicken stock to pan juices and bring to the boil.
Strain into a sauceboat and serve with chicken, roast potatoes and
green vegetables.

CHICKEN AND VEGETABLE STIR-FRY

500 g (1 lb) chicken strips
2 tablespoons canola oil
1 clove garlic, crushed
1 cm (½ in) piece fresh ginger, finely chopped
6 shallots (scallions), sliced into 1 cm/½ in lengths
2 tablespoons oyster sauce
½ teaspoon chicken stock powder
60 ml (2 fl oz) cup water
1 medium carrot, chopped
1 red capsicum (bell pepper), cut into strips
225 g (8 oz) canned water chestnuts, drained
225 g (8 oz) canned baby corn pieces, drained
200 g (7 oz) mange tout/snow peas, trimmed
60 g (2 oz) cup bean sprouts

Serves 4

Trim any visible fat from the chicken. Heat oil in a wok, add garlic, ginger and spring onions and stir-fry for 1 minute, then add chicken and stir-fry until cooked through. Remove the chicken and spring onions from the wok.

Mix together the oyster sauce, stock powder and water and add to the wok. Add the carrot and red pepper and cook, lifting vegetables from the bottom and turning over continuously for 2 minutes. Add remaining vegetables and continue stirring for 2 minutes.

Return the chicken and spring onions to the pan and toss through vegetables for 2 minutes to reheat. Pile onto a platter and serve immediately.

CHICKEN SCHNITZEL SLIDERS

60 g (2 oz) panko breadcrumbs
salt and pepper, to taste
2 eggs
500 g (1 lb) chicken breast fillets, cut into pieces to fit
    buns
1 tablespoon olive oil
baby spinach
2 tomatoes, sliced
whole egg mayonnaise or some onion relish
12 slider buns of your choice

Makes 12

In a shallow bowl, combine the panko breadcrumbs, salt and
pepper. In another bowl, beat the two eggs. Dip the chicken
pieces in the beaten egg, shake off excess then dip into the
panko breadcrumbs.

In a non-stick frying pan, heat the oil on a medium-high heat and
cook the schnitzels until golden brown for 4–5 minutes each side.

Slice your buns in half lengthwise and toast.

To assemble your sliders, spread on the mayonnaise on the
bottom half of the buns, add a piece of schnitzel, some baby
spinach, a slice of tomato and the top of the bun. Hold together with
cocktail stick.

SOUTHERN FRIED CHICKEN

1 chicken
60 g (2 oz) flour
salt and freshly ground black pepper, to taste
1 teaspoon paprika (optional)
125 g (4 oz) butter or olive oil, for frying
gravy, to serve

Serves 4–6

Disjoint the chicken and soak it in salted water for 10 minutes.
Shake off excess water.

In a large paper bag, shake flour, salt and pepper and paprika
(if using) together to mix. Put chicken pieces in the bag and shake
thoroughly to coat.

In a large frying pan, heat butter and fry all chicken pieces
together over a high heat until golden brown on one side.
Turn pieces over, lower heat and continue to fry, turning
occasionally, until meat is tender (30–40 minutes, depending on
size of chicken).

Drain and serve hot with gravy or other sauces to suit.

CHICKEN DRUMETTES

60 ml (2 fl oz) olive oil
60 ml (2 fl oz) tomato sauce
2 tablespoons honey
1 tablespoon barbecue sauce
1 tablespoon Dijon mustard
3 teaspoons Worcestershire sauce
2 cloves garlic, crushed
1 kg (2 lb) chicken drumettes
parsley, to garnish

Makes 18-20

Combine olive oil, tomato sauce, honey, barbecue sauce, Dijon mustard, Worcestershire sauce and garlic in a shallow dish.

Add chicken and coat well in mixture. Cover with plastic wrap and place in the refrigerator to marinate for 2–3 hours.

Preheat the oven to 200°C (400°F). Line a baking tray with foil. Place chicken on a rack over the baking tray. Bake in the oven for 30–35 minutes or until cooked. Garnish with parsley, to serve.

MEAT

POT ROASTING

This is one of the simplest ways of cooking a joint of meat. It is a slow method of cooking which makes tough meat moist, tender and tasty. It is important to have the right type of pot or casserole dish. It should be of thick iron, enameled cast iron, aluminum or flameproof pottery, and big enough to hold a joint comfortably and with a close-fitting lid.

First, the meat is browned all over in the pot, using 1–2 tablespoons of olive oil. Then add an onion stuck with 2–3 cloves, a bouquet garni and salt and pepper. Don't add liquid unless the recipe tells you to; it will usually not be more than 75 ml (⅓ cup) stock or wine. You can also add a thick layer of vegetables – whole potatoes, carrots, turnips, onions – into the pan. Cut the vegetables into pieces so that they will be well done but not overcooked when the meat is done.

Put the lid on and place the pot over a very low heat or into a slow oven (150°C/300°F), allowing approximately 30 minutes per 500 g (1 lb).

Beef

Allow about 25–30 minutes per 500 g (1 lb) and 25–30 minutes over, depending upon how well done you like it.

Chicken

Allow 20–25 minutes per 500 g (1 lb) and 20–25 minutes over. Remember to weigh the chicken after you have stuffed it.

Lamb, mutton, veal

Allow 35–40 minutes per 500 g (1 lb) and 35–40 minutes over.

GRILLING

Grilling requires a certain amount of attention. Heat the grill first until it is red hot. While it is heating, also heat the grill rack in the grill pan underneath. If raw meat is placed on a hot grill rack it will not stick to it during cooking.

Brush the meat lightly with olive oil. Do not salt it; this causes the juices to run out, and you will lose some of the natural flavor and nutritional value of the meat. Place the prepared meat under the red-hot grill and cook until it changes color from red-pink to brown (1–2 minutes). This means the surface of the meat has seared and the juices are sealed in. Turn the meat over and sear the other side, then continue to grill for the required cooking time, or until the meat is cooked to your taste. Turn the meat with tongs or two spoons to avoid piercing the seal. If you need to slow the cooking down, move the grill pan down, further away from the red hot grill, rather than reducing the temperature of the grill.

Cooking times for grilling meat depend on the cut, the thickness and your own taste. When a cooked steak is pressed with your fingers it feels like a sponge if it's rare, is firmer and less spongy if it's medium, and is quite firm, with no give, when well done. Grilled steaks should be served immediately.

Cuts	Degree	Grilling Times in minutes
rump steak	rare	6–7
750 g (2.5 cm/1 in) thick	medium rare	8–10
serves 3–4	well done	14–16
sirloin or rib steak	rare	5
2–2.5 cm (¾–1 in) thick	medium rare	6–7
serves 1	well done	9–10
minute steak	rare	1
(thin slice of rib steak)	medium rare	2–3
1 cm (½ in) thick		
serves 1		
t-bone steak	rare	7–8
3.5–5 cm (1½–2 in) thick	medium rare	8–10
serves 2–3		
porterhouse steak		
3.5–5 cm (1½–2 in) thick	rare	7–8
serves 1–2	medium rare	8–10
fillet steak	rare	6
2.5–3.5 cm (1–1½ in) thick	medium rare to well done	7–8
serves 1		

Cuts	Degree	Grilling Times in minutes
tournedos	rare	6
2.5–3.5 cm	medium rare to well done	7–8
(1–1½ in) thick		
serves 1		
Chateaubriand	rare to medium rare	16–20
8–10 cm (3¼–4 in) thick		
serves 2		
pork chops	well done	15–20
lamb chops		8–10
sausages	thick	10–15
	thin	8–10
kidneys		10
bacon	rasher	3–4

FRYING

Frying is a quick method of cooking. There are two methods of frying: deep and shallow. Meat is seldom deep fried. Steak, chops, cutlets and veal cordon bleu are often shallow fried. Meat is often shallow fried as a first stage – this is done when you are making stews, braising or pot roasting.

When frying meat, choose the fat or oil which most complements the natural flavor of the meat: butter is best for juicy fillet steak and delicate wiener schnitzel; a mixture of butter and oil is ideal for most meats, and the oil stops the butter burning; olive oil gives an authentic flavor to Mediterranean meat dishes; and peanut oil is used for Oriental meat dishes, such as stir-fries.

Frying is not always done in a frying pan in meat cookery; it's often done in a saucepan or a flameproof casserole. Whatever is used, make sure it has a heavy base which will distribute the heat evenly. This will help ensure that the meat doesn't burn or stick.

When you are shallow frying meat in a frying pan, the fat should cover the base of the pan, and in some recipes it should come halfway up the meat, so that the sides are completely cooked (with crumbed cutlets, for example). Turn the food once only and remember that the surface of the food which is fried first is the most attractive, and so should be served uppermost.

If the piece of meat you are cooking is thick (more than 2.5 cm/1 in thick), cook it on a moderate heat after first browning it on a high heat. The brown sediment left in the pan after frying meat is the concentrated meat juices. To make a quick gravy from this, first pour off the excess fat. Then reheat the frying pan adding a little water, stock or wine. When the liquid has reduced to a gravy consistency, pour it over the meat.

STEWING

Stewing is cooking food slowly and gently in liquid. Meat can be stewed either on top of the stove or in the oven. During stewing, the liquid should simmer gently, with bubbles just breaking the surface. Meat for stewing is usually from less tender cuts. It will have a slight marbling of fat or gristle, and requires long, slow cooking. During the stewing the gristle is changed into gelatin, which means the meat becomes tender; the fat gives flavor to the stew. If you allow the liquid to boil rapidly, the meat will become tough.

Meat stews can be either brown or white. In a brown stew the meat is browned in fat first, and some flour is often added and browned to give extra color and flavor. Vegetables may also be browned to add to the color and flavor. Enough stock is added to come to just below the top of the meat. The pan or casserole is then covered, and the stew is cooked slowly on top of the stove or in the oven, until the meat is tender. A flameproof casserole is ideal for cooking stews, but you can do the preliminary frying in a frying pan or large saucepan and then transfer the meat to an ovenproof casserole. Stews are usually served direct from the casserole.

In a white stew (often called a fricassee), the meat is not browned. Instead, it is often blanched first to whiten it and remove strong flavors. A white stew is cooked on top of the stove and is thickened after the meat is cooked.

BOILING

Boiling is cooking food covered with water at boiling point. In the case of boiling meat, put the joint into boiling, salted water and bring it back to the boil to seal the outside and seal in the meat juices. Then reduce the heat and cook the meat in simmering water until tender. Allow 20–25 minutes per 500 g (1 lb) and 20–25 minutes over.

SAUTÉING

Meat used for sautéing must be young, tender and of best quality, such as pork and veal fillet. Sautéing is frying meat lightly in a small quantity of butter and/or oil to seal in the juices. A small quantity of stock or wine is added during the cooking process to come level with the top of the meat, and this is simmered a little to reduce the sauce and concentrate the flavor. The sauce can be thickened at this point if you prefer it thicker.

If you want to create a sauce for your meat whilst cooking it, a sauté pan should be used. A sauté pan is a 7 cm (2½ in) deep, straight-sided, heavy frying pan with a lid. The wide base allows room for browning, and for quick reduction of the sauce. The lid is used if you need to slow down reduction of the sauce, and ensures complete cooking of the meat because it keeps the moisture and heat in the pan. A deep-frying pan with a lid can also be used.

BRAISING

Braising is an ideal method of cooking cheaper, tougher cuts of meat. Braising is a combination of steaming and baking: the meat is cooked in a heavy pot on top of a bed of vegetables, with liquid coming a quarter of the way up the side of the meat. Braising can be done on top of the stove or in the oven in a heavy flameproof cast-iron casserole dish. A whole joint can be braised, or meat can be cut into 5 cm (2 in) cubes and braised, in the case of ragouts.

First, brown the meat in fat in the pot. Put it aside. Then sauté a mixture of root vegetables, cut into chunky pieces, gently in the fat, with the lid on, for 10–15 minutes. This mixture of vegetables is called a mirepoix, and is not served with the meat – it is discarded after the cooking. Place the meat on top of the vegetables and add the liquid and herbs, then leave the dish to simmer for 2–3 hours. Serve the meat with the gravy strained and poured over it.

STEAMING

Steaming is a long, slow, moist method of cooking – the food is surrounded by steam rising from boiling water. Tough joints of meat are often steamed before they are roasted, as steaming will make them more tender. Large pieces of meat can be steamed in a steamer placed over a pan of boiling water. Small cuts of tender meat can be cooked between two heatproof plates over a pan of boiling water. Steamed meat is easily digested, and none of the flavor or food value is lost.

CASSEROLE COOKING

Casserole cooking is similar to pot roasting, but the meat is cut up and cooked in liquid and the food is usually served in the dish it was cooked in. Other ingredients – vegetables, flavorings and herbs – are added to the meat, and it is usually cooked in the oven. This method of cooking requires very little attention and is ideal for both tender and tough cuts of meat, though the latter take longer to cook.

CARVING MEAT

Keep your knives sharp for efficient carving. A steel, for sharpening your knives, and a carving fork which has a guard are also essential pieces of equipment.

Leg of lamb

This method is simple, and gives a high yield of sliced meat.
Wrap a cloth or napkin around the bone or handle of the leg.
Hold the leg by the handle and rest it on a carving plate at an angle
of 45°, with the meatier side uppermost. Starting midway on the
joint, slice the meat down at an oblique angle. Slice down again at
an opposite oblique angle and remove the wedge shaped piece of
meat. Continue slicing down each side of the cut. Slices should be
about 3 mm (⅛ in) thick. Keep slicing until you reach the leg bone.
Turn the leg over and repeat the process.

Loin of lamb

Lie the joint on its side. Place your carving fork firmly in the joint
and slice straight down between the bones, into thick slices.

Rolled rib and rolled sirloin of beef

Method 1: Using a fork with a safety guard, hold the joint flat on the
carving plate. Slice meat across the grain towards the fork.

Method 2: Hold the joint on its side with a fork. Slice downwards,
towards the carving plate.

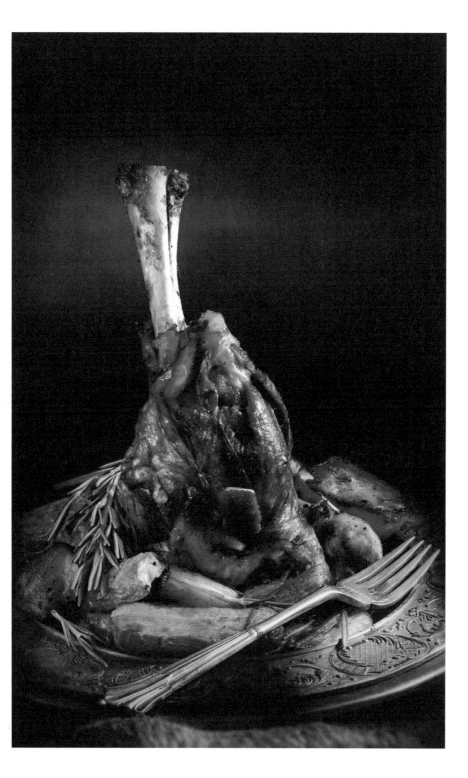

BEEF STROGANOFF

90 g (3 oz) butter
1 large onion, thinly sliced
250 g (8 oz) mushrooms, peeled and sliced
750 g (1½ lb) fillet steak, trimmed of fat and cut into
    thin strips
1½ teaspoons salt
freshly ground black pepper, to taste
pinch of nutmeg
300 g (10 oz) sour cream
parsley, chopped, to garnish

Serves 4

Melt 60 g (2 oz) butter in a heavy frying pan and sauté the onion
until soft. Add mushrooms and cook for 5 minutes. Place mixture in
a bowl and keep warm.

Melt remaining butter in pan and quickly brown beef strips on all
sides. Do this stage in two lots unless you have a very large frying
pan. Take pan off the heat and add onion, mushrooms, salt, pepper
and nutmeg. Stir well to blend, then replace pan over a medium
heat and pour in sour cream. Stir gently until heated through.
Do not allow sauce to boil.

Serve with boiled rice, cooked cabbage or coleslaw
(see page 50).

BEEF BOURGUIGNON

2 tablespoons flour
1 kg (2 lb) stewing beef,
   chuck, blade or shin,
   diced
90 g (3 oz) butter
1 tablespoon tomato paste
2 garlic cloves, crushed
750 ml (1½ pints)
   burgundy

625 ml (20 fl oz)
   beef stock
salt and pepper, to taste
1 bouquet garni
60 g (2 oz) pickled pork or
   bacon, diced
12 small onions
2 carrots, sliced
12 button mushrooms
chopped parsley, to garnish

Serves 6

Preheat oven to 165°C (330°F). Brown flour in a saucepan on
medium heat for a few minutes until golden brown. Sprinkle diced
beef with flour, then fry in a large pot with the butter for 5 minutes.
Add tomato paste and garlic and cook for a further 5 minutes.
Add burgundy and stock, season lightly with salt and pepper and
add bouquet garni.

   Cover and cook in the oven for 2½–3 hours, or until tender.

   In a frying pan, fry pickled pork or bacon lightly. Add onions
and carrots and cook over a moderate heat until evenly browned.
Add pork or bacon and the mushrooms to the pot about 15 minutes
before cooking is finished. Adjust consistency and seasoning if
necessary and serve hot, sprinkled with chopped parsley.

Note: The traditional recipe has 2 tablespoons of brandy added in
the final stage along with the mushrooms.

BEEF SLIDERS

1 tablespoon butter
1 small onion, finely diced
1 clove garlic, minced
500 g (1 lb) best-quality ground/minced beef you can
   afford
1 egg
1 teaspoon Dijon mustard
1 teaspoon Worcestershire sauce
salt and pepper
1 tablespoon olive oil
iceberg lettuce, sliced
Spanish onion, finely sliced
1–2 tomatoes, sliced
pickles, to serve
12 slider buns of your choosing

Makes 12

In a non-stick frying pan on a medium heat melt the butter and cook
the onion and garlic until golden and allow to cool.

Place meat in a large bowl and mix in the cooked onion, garlic, egg,
Worcestershire sauce and season with salt and pepper. Roll into
small balls and flatten the patties to fit your buns. Heat the oil in a
frying pan and cook for about 20 minutes until firm to the touch or
cooked to your liking.

Slice the buns in half lengthways.

Spread the bottom halves of the buns with tomato sauce. Add on
a cooked patty, some lettuce, onion, tomato and the top of the bun.
Hold the buns together with cocktail sticks and serve while hot.

PERFECT STEAK

steak of choice
2 teaspoons crushed garlic
2 teaspoons oil
salt and pepper

GARLIC BUTTER
55 g (2 oz) butter
1 teaspoon crushed garlic
1 tablespoon parsley flakes
2 teaspoons lemon juice

Makes 12

Combine the garlic butter ingredients. Spoon into a small pot and
set aside. Bring the steaks to room temperature.

Mix the garlic, oil and salt and pepper together.

Rub onto both sides of the steak. Stand for 10–15 minutes at
room temperature. Heat the barbecue or frypan until hot and oil the
grill bars.

Place the steak on the barbecue or pan and sear for 1 minute on
each side. Move the steak to the cooler part of the barbecue or pan
to continue cooking over a moderate heat, or turn the heat down.
If the heat cannot be reduced then elevate the steaks on a wire
cake rack placed on the grill bars or in the oven on low. Cook for
a total time of 5–6 minutes for rare, 7–10 minutes for medium and
10–14 minutes for well done. Turn during cooking.

Serve on a heated steak plate and top with a dollop of garlic
butter. Serve with potatoes.

BRAISED LAMB SHANKS

2 tablespoons olive oil
4 lamb shanks
1 onion, chopped
1 clove garlic (optional), crushed
1 carrot, diced
120 g (4 oz) celery, diced
200 g (7 oz) skinned, chopped tomatoes or
    tinned tomatoes
1 teaspoon salt
¼ teaspoon freshly ground black pepper
½ teaspoon sugar
60 ml (2 fl oz) beef stock or water
1 teaspoon Worcestershire sauce

Serves 4

Heat oil in a frying pan and brown lamb shanks, over a moderately
high heat. Pour off most of the oil and reduce heat. Add onion,
garlic (if used), carrot and celery and cook until onion is soft.

Stir in tomatoes, salt, pepper, sugar, stock and Worcestershire
sauce. Spoon some of the vegetable mixture over the shanks.
Place a lid on the pan and simmer for 2 hours, or until tender.
Adjust flavor before serving.

Serve with mashed potatoes and steamed vegetables.

CHILLI CON CARNE

2 tablespoon olive oil
1 large onion, chopped
1 green capsicum (bell pepper), seeds and pith removed
  and chopped
1 stick celery, chopped
1 tablespoon chilli powder (optional)
½ teaspoon salt
pinch of cayenne pepper
2 teaspoons paprika
500 g (1 lb) minced or diced beef
250 g (8 oz) tomatoes or 625 ml (21 fl oz) tomato pulp
250 g (8 oz) cooked kidney beans or soaked and
  cooked haricot beans
150 ml (5 fl oz) water
Add cheese and shallots if desired

Serves 4

Heat oil in a saucepan. Add onion, capsicum and celery and fry until
just tender, then add other ingredients. Bring just to the boil, then
lower the heat and cook gently for about 55 minutes (for minced
meat) or 1¼ hours (for diced meat). Stir halfway through cooking,
and add a little more water if necessary.

   Serve in individual bowls or a large bowl with cheese and
shallots if desired on top.

Note: Some people like to add 60 g (2 oz) cooked rice to the recipe.

IRISH STEW

1 kg (2 lb) potatoes, peeled
salt and pepper, to taste
1 kg (2 lb) lamb neck chops, trimmed of fat
500 g (1 lb) white onions, thickly sliced
bunch of herbs (parsley, thyme, rosemary)
1 bay leaf
625 ml (1¼ pints) beef stock (see page 376)
1 tablespoon extra parsley, finely chopped, to garnish

Serves 5–6

Preheat oven to 165°C (330°F). Cut 3–4 potatoes into thick slices and cut remaining potatoes in halves.

Place sliced potatoes in an ovenproof casserole dish and season with salt and pepper. Cover with meat, then add onions and halved potatoes, and season again. Add herbs, bay leaf and stock.

Cover casserole dish and cook in the oven for 2–2½, hours or until meat is tender. Remove herbs and bay leaf from casserole and sprinkle with chopped parsley before serving.

FILLET MIGNON

4 bacon rashers, rind removed
4 slices of fillet steak, 3.5 cm (2½ in) thick
salt and freshly ground black pepper, to taste
parsley butter

Serves 4

Wrap a bacon rasher around each fillet and secure with toothpick.
Preheat grill to hot and brush rack with oil. Place fillet under grill
rack 8 cm (3¼ in) below heat.

Grill for 3–4 minutes on each side for rare steak, 2 minutes
longer each side for medium rare steak. Turn fillets gently so you
don't pierce the meat and let the juices escape. Season with salt
and pepper and serve immediately.

Garnish with parsley butter and serve immediately with
roast potatoes.

STEAK SANDWICH

500 g (1 lb) rump or sirloin steak (whichever you prefer)
pepper, freshly ground, to taste
salt, to taste

SANDWICH
loaf of sliced sourdough
rocket (arugula)
2 tomatoes, sliced
caramelized onion, to serve
mayonnaise, to serve

Serves 4

Prepare barbecue or fry pan for direct heat cooking on a high.

Season the steak with salt and pepper on both sides place the steak on the grill or fry pan and cook to your liking.

Rest the steak while you toast sourdough on the grill.

Slice the steak then butter one side of the toasted sourdough. Add the mayonnaise, rocket and tomato the season with salt and pepper to taste and top with the sliced steak and caramelized onion.

Place the other slice of sourdough on top and enjoy.

STEAK WITH PEPPER SAUCE

500 g rump steak, trimmed
freshly ground black pepper
salt, to taste

PEPPER SAUCE
15 g (½ oz) fresh parsley, chopped
15 g (½ oz) fresh chives, chopped
knob of butter
60 ml (2 fl oz) cup cream
Pepper to taste

Serves 4

Prepare the barbecue and ensure it has a high heat or a hot heavy duty fry pan.

Place the rump steak on the grill or pan and lightly sprinkle with pepper. Cook until lightly browned, then turn and lightly sprinkle the other side with pepper.

To make the sauce, fry the parsley and chives with a knob of butter in a pan. Then add the cream and pepper. If you want a lot of sauce, add all the cream. If only a little sauce is required, add only half the quantity.

Serve the rump steak with sauce on the side, season with salt to taste.

BEEF CARPACCIO

500 g (1 lb) beef fillet
3 tablespoons extra-virgin olive oil
salt and freshly ground black pepper
125 g (4 oz) rocket (arugula)
1 tablespoon balsamic vinegar
pecorino cheese shavings

Serves 4

With a sharp knife, slice the beef into 5 mm-thick slices.

Lightly oil a sheet of baking paper and season it lightly with salt and freshly ground black pepper.

Arrange 4 slices of beef on this, approximately 5 cm (2 in) apart. Place another oiled piece of baking paper on top, and gently pound the meat until it has spread out to at least twice its former size. Repeat with remaining meat slices.

Refrigerate until needed.

Place rocket in the centre of a plate, arrange the beef slices around the rocket. Drizzle with balsamic vinegar and remaining olive oil. Serve, topped with shavings of pecorino cheese and more black pepper.

LESLEY'S MAGIC RISSOLES

1 egg
60 ml (2 fl oz) milk
750 g (1½ lb) fine mince meat or chicken mince
60 g (2 oz) breadcrumbs
1 tablespoon red wine
1 carrot, grated
1 zucchini, grated
1 onion, grated
1 teaspoon soy sauce
dash of Worcestershire sauce
60 g (2 oz) flour
1 tablespoon butter

Serves 4

Beat egg and milk together in a large bowl. Add mince and all other ingredients except flour and butter and mix well.

Spread flour onto a cutting board. Form meat mixture into balls and roll in flour. Then flatten (with a spatula or knife) into rissoles and place on greaseproof paper. Continue until all mixture has been used.

Heat butter in a frying pan over a low heat. Place rissoles in the frying pan and cook for 5 minutes, or until the bottom is golden brown, then turn and continue to cook for 10 minutes or until golden brown on the other side and cooked through.

Serve with vegetables and mashed potato (see page 131).

MOUSSAKA

4 tablespoons olive oil
2 onions, finely chopped
2 cloves garlic, crushed
500 g (1 lb) lamb
   forequarter, chopped
   or minced
185 g (6 oz) mushrooms,
   chopped
500 g (1 lb) tomatoes,
   skinned, seeded
   and chopped
2 tablespoons
   tomato paste
150 ml (5 fl oz) beef
   stock (see page 376)
2 medium-sized
   eggplants, cut into 1 cm
   (½ in) slices
125 g (4 oz) plain (all-
   purpose) flour
salt and pepper, to taste
90 g (3 oz) Parmesan
   cheese, grated
1 tablespoon parsley,
   chopped

Serves 6

Preheat oven to 200°C (400°F). Heat 1 tablespoon olive oil in a
large saucepan till hot, then sauté onion and garlic until soft, but not
colored. Add lamb and fry until lightly browned. Add mushrooms
and tomatoes and cook for 5 minutes. Add tomato paste and stock.
Cook for a further 5 minutes.

   Roll eggplant slices in flour. Heat remaining oil in a frying
pan, and fry eggplant slices on both sides. Drain on absorbent
paper. Line the base of an ovenproof casserole dish with slices of
eggplant. Pour over some of the lamb mixture, season with salt
and pepper and sprinkle with parsley. Cover with another layer of
eggplant and repeat the process until casserole dish is full, finishing
with a layer of eggplant. Sprinkle with Parmesan cheese and cook
in the oven until golden brown – approximately 10–15 minutes.
Serve sprinkled with chopped parsley.

Variation: Before adding the Parmesan cheese, pour over a layer
of béchamel sauce (see page 354) and cook in the oven for
approximately 15–20 minutes.

MEATLOAF

750 g (1½ lb) minced beef
45 g (1½ oz) breadcrumbs
1 onion, grated
75 g (2½ oz) carrot, grated
2 tablespoons capsicum (bell pepper) (optional),
  seeds and pith removed and finely chopped
60 ml (2 fl oz) tomato purée
60 ml (2 fl oz) milk
1 egg, beaten
2 tablespoons parsley, chopped
½ teaspoon mixed herbs
1½ teaspoons salt
freshly ground black pepper, to taste
chopped parsley, to garnish

Serves 4–6

Preheat oven to 180°C (350°F). Place minced beef in a large bowl.
In another bowl, blend together the breadcrumbs, onion, carrot,
capsicum (if used), tomato purée and milk. Stir in egg, herbs and
salt and pepper. Combine this mixture with the minced beef.

Spoon meat mixture into a greased standard-sized loaf tin and
bake in the oven for 1 hour. Drain off liquid, unmold onto a warm
serving platter and serve garnished with parsley and accompanied
by steamed vegetables and potatoes.

Variation:
Tomato–Cheese Loaf: Unmold meatloaf as above, lay slices of
tomato and cheese on top and return to the oven until cheese melts
and browns slightly.

BLUE CHEESE STUFFED HAMBURGER

1 tablespoon butter
1 brown onion, finely diced
1 garlic clove, crushed
1 kg (2 lbs) beef mince
½ teaspoon salt
½ teaspoon cracked pepper
1 teaspoon Worcestershire sauce
1 tablespoon barbecue sauce
30 g panko breadcrumbs
1 egg
250 g (8 oz) blue cheese (cut into five slices)
5 soft burger buns of your choice, halved
1 baby cos lettuce
2–3 tomatoes, sliced
aïoli or caramelized onions, to serve

Serves 4–6

Melt the butter in a frying pan over medium heat. Add the onion and garlic and sweat until golden. Allow to cool. Combined the mince, onion and garlic, salt, pepper, Worcestershire sauce, barbecue sauce, panko breadcrumbs and egg in a bowl. Mix by hand until well mixed. Separate the mix into five equal balls.

Separate each ball again into two equal balls and place a piece of blue cheese into the centre and mold into a patty. Flatten and ensure each patty is well sealed around the edges. Place the patties on a medium–high barbecue flatplate or frypan and cook the patties for 3–4 minutes on each side or done to your liking. Spread the top half of the burger bun with aïoli or caramelized onion. Add the patty, then the lettuce leaves and tomato. Serve hot (but make sure you warn everyone about the hot cheese filling).

SESAME LAMB

1 tablespoon oil
2 medium onions, diced
1 carrot, diced
1 parsnip, diced
2 teaspoons garlic, chopped
3 bacon rashers, diced
1 kg (2 lbs) lamb leg meat, diced
250 ml (8 fl oz) red wine
1 teaspoon mixed herbs
3 bay leaves
salt and freshly ground black pepper, to taste
8 mushrooms, sliced or diced
fresh coriander (cilantro) leaves, chopped, to taste
2 tablespoons sesame seeds

Serves 6

Heat oil in a frying pan and fry onion, carrot, parsnip and garlic
for 5 minutes. Add bacon and cook for a few more minutes.
Add lamb, red wine, mixed herbs, bay leaves and salt and
pepper. Bring mixture to the boil (add a little water if necessary),
then reduce heat and simmer for 30 minutes. Add mushrooms,
coriander and sesame seeds and simmer for a further 15 minutes.

Serve with rice or potatoes. Garnish with a little fresh coriander.

Note: You can 'heat up' the dish by adding a small amount of hot
chilli sauce.

PORK WITH MARSALA

500–750 g (1–1½ lb) pork fillets, trimmed of fat
flour, seasoned with salt and
   freshly ground black pepper, for coating
3 tablespoons olive oil
salt and freshly ground black pepper, to taste
1 tablespoon water
2 tablespoons plain (all-purpose) flour
125 ml (4 fl oz) Marsala
30 g (1 oz) butter

Serves 4

Slice pork lengthways, almost through, so they form a butterfly
fillet. Lay fillets open between 2 sheets of plastic cling wrap, and
flatten with a meat mallet. Cut meat into pieces about 10 x 5 cm
(4 x 2 in). Pound again until very thin, taking care not to break the
slices. Dust lightly with seasoned flour.

Heat oil in a pan and brown meat for 2 minutes on each
side over a high heat. Sprinkle lightly with salt and generously
with pepper, then remove meat from the pan and arrange slices
overlapping on a warm serving dish. Keep warm.

Add water to pan, then add flour and stir in, scraping up the
crusty meat and flour leftovers. Pour in Marsala and stir until sauce
is thickened and smooth, then add butter. When butter is melted,
pour hot sauce over meat and serve.

MINUTE STEAKS

8 pieces fillet steak,
2.5 cm (1 in) thick,
trimmed of fat
salt and black pepper,
to taste
250 g (8 oz) butter
for frying

STEAK CHAMPIGNON
500 g (1 lb) mushrooms,
sliced
315 ml (10 ½ fl oz)
fresh cream

STEAK DIANE
4 tablespoons parsley,
finely chopped
16 cloves garlic, crushed
8 teaspoons
Worcestershire sauce

PAPRIKA STEAK
pinch of paprika
8 tablespoons brandy

Serves 8

Pound steaks with a meat mallet until they are 5 mm (¼ in) thick.
Rub with salt and pepper.

Melt 30 g (1 oz) butter in a frying pan for each steak.
When butter is sizzling, add steak and fry for 1 minute on each side.
Serve each steak as it is cooked, and spoon over the pan juices.

Variations:

Steak Champignon: Add 60 g (2 oz) mushrooms to pan as you
cook steak. When turning steak, add 1 tablespoon cream. Lift out
steaks and mushrooms. Heat pan juices for 10 seconds over high
heat, stirring continuously. Pour over steaks and serve.

Steak Diane: As steak starts to sizzle, sprinkle with chopped
parsley and 1 crushed clove garlic. As steak is turned, add
1 teaspoon Worcestershire sauce, a little more parsley and
1 more crushed clove of garlic. Cook for 1 minute on second side
and serve.

Paprika Steak: Sprinkle both sides of steak with paprika before
cooking. Once steaks are cooked, add 1 tablespoon of brandy to pan
for each steak, just before serving. Ignite and serve.

POT ROAST

3 tablespoons butter
1.5–2 kg (3–4 lb) corner piece topside steak
2 large carrots, peeled and cut into chunks
2 large parsnips, peeled and cut into chunks
5–6 onions, peeled and cut into chunks
salt and freshly ground black pepper, to taste
180 ml (6 fl oz) water

Serves 5–6

Heat butter in a large flameproof casserole dish (use one that has a tight-fitting lid) and brown meat evenly on all sides. Remove meat from dish and set aside. Brown vegetables in remaining fat, remove from dish and set aside.

Put meat back in casserole dish, season with salt and pepper and add 2 tablespoons boiling water. Cover casserole with greased paper or aluminum foil and put the lid on. Cook over a gentle heat for 2½ hours, or until meat is tender, adding 2 tablespoons boiling water to casserole every 30 minutes. Add vegetables 1½ hours before cooking time is completed.

Serve with new potatoes and gravy from casserole.

ROAST LEG OF LAMB

1 x 1.5 kg (3 lb) leg of lamb
salt, to taste
freshly ground black pepper, to taste
2 cloves garlic, sliced
2–3 sprigs fresh rosemary

Serves 4–6

Preheat oven to 165°C (330°F).

Place lamb in a roasting pan and rub the meat with salt and pepper. Make cuts into meat and press slices of garlic inside. Place sprigs of rosemary on top of lamb.

Roast lamb in the oven for 1 hour and 40 minutes. Basting is not required unless the lamb is very young and has little fat. Season with salt after roasting and let the joint stand in a warm place for 15 minutes before carving.

Serve with roast vegetables, gravy, mint sauce (see page 369) or mint jelly.

ROAST PORK

1 x 3 kg (6½ lb) loin leg of pork
salt, to taste
apple sauce, to serve

Serves 8–12

Preheat oven to 245°C (480°F). Rub pork with salt and place in a
roasting pan. Cook pork in oven for 30 minutes to crisp crackling,
then reduce heat to moderately slow (165°C/330°F) and cook for
3 hours. Continue to baste throughout cooking time.

When pork is cooked, place in a carving tray and keep warm.
Make gravy from pan juices.

Serve roast pork with apple sauce, roast potatoes and
roast vegetables.

RACK OF LAMB

1 rib rack of 6 lamb cutlets, trimmed of fat
pinch of salt
mint jelly or mint sauce (see page 369)

Serves 3

Preheat oven to 165°C (325°F). Rub lamb with salt. Place lamb on
a rack in a roasting pan and cook in the oven for about 45 minutes.
Carve (on a board) into 6 cutlets. Place 2 cutlets on each plate,
with frills placed on each bone. Serve with mint jelly or mint sauce.

ROAST BEEF

1 x 1.5 kg (3 lb) rolled sirloin of beef
salt and freshly ground black pepper, to taste
butter or olive oil, for roasting

Serves 6

Preheat oven to 165°C (330°F). Rub meat with salt and pepper and place in a roasting pan, fat side up. If the joint has little fat, add 1–2 tablespoons butter or oil to the pan. Place beef in the oven and cook for 2 hours.

Remove roast beef to a hot carving platter and leave to stand in a warm place for 15–30 minutes before carving. This makes it easier to carve the meat.

Serve with Yorkshire Pudding (see page 341), roast vegetables (pumpkin or parsnip), and with gravy (see page 353), horseradish cream (see page 364) or mustard.

SHEPHERD'S PIE

1 tablespoon olive oil
1 onion, finely chopped
2 tomatoes, skinned and chopped
375 g (12 oz) beef mince, cooked
good pinch of mixed herbs
salt and pepper, to taste
315 ml (10 ½ fl oz) beef stock (see page 376)
500 g (1 lb) mashed potato (see page 131)
30 g (1 oz) butter

Serves 4

Preheat oven to 200°C (375°F). In a frying pan, heat olive oil and fry
onion for 3 minutes. Add tomatoes and meat and heat together for
2–3 minutes. Stir in herbs, seasoning and stock – add less stock if
you desire a thicker consistency.

Put meat mixture into a pie dish and cover with mashed potato.
Use a fork to score the edges, or create any other design you like.
Dot tiny pieces of butter around on the potato to help it brown.
Bake in the centre of the oven until the top is crisp and brown.

STEAK DIANE

4 slices of fillet steak cut 2.5 cm (1 in) thick
30 g (1 oz) butter
2 cloves garlic, crushed
salt and freshly ground black pepper, to taste
1 tablespoon tomato sauce
1 teaspoon Worcestershire sauce
60 ml (2 fl oz) water
1 teaspoon cornflour, mixed with a little cold water

Serves 4

Slit steaks horizontally through to the centre and open out meat to create a butterfly fillet. Flatten steaks with the side of a meat mallet to 5 mm (¼ in) thickness.

Melt half the butter in a heavy frying pan, add 1 crushed garlic clove and fry the steaks quickly – about 40 seconds on each side for rare steak and 1 minute each side for medium steak. Add remaining butter and garlic to the pan when cooking the rest of the steaks (most frying pans will probably hold only two steaks at a time). Season cooked steaks with salt and pepper and keep aside on a warm platter.

Add sauces and water to frying pan and stir into pan juices over a medium heat. Thicken with cornflour paste and bring to the boil. Pour sauce over steaks.

Serve with new potatoes and a tossed green salad.

SPICY LAMB CURRY

1 medium onion, chopped
2 cloves garlic, crushed
¼ teaspoon chilli powder
60 ml (2 fl oz) lemon juice
1 tablespoon curry powder
½ teaspoon celery salt
½ teaspoon ground ginger
1.5 kg (3 lb) lamb chops, cut into 2.5 cm (1 in) cubes
2 tablespoons olive oil
2 medium onions, chopped
2 cloves garlic, crushed
½ teaspoon mustard seeds
½ teaspoon cumin
1 teaspoon turmeric
1 teaspoon paprika
½ teaspoon garam masala
1 medium tomato, peeled and chopped
250 ml (8 fl oz) chicken stock (see page 377)
125 ml (4 fl oz) coconut cream

Serves 6

Combine onion, garlic, chilli powder, lemon juice, curry powder,
celery salt, ground ginger and lamb cubes in a bowl, and stir until
lamb is evenly coated. Cover, and refrigerate for 1 hour.

Preheat oven to 180°C (350°F). Heat oil in a large saucepan
and add onions and garlic. Sauté for 1 minute. Add lamb and cook,
stirring, until browned. Add mustard seeds, cumin, turmeric,
paprika, garam masala, tomato and chicken stock, and cook for
5 minutes. Spoon into a large ovenproof dish and cover.

Bake in the oven for 1½ hours, or until tender. Stir in coconut
cream just before serving. Serve with boiled or steamed rice.

TASTY ROAST BEEF

2 teaspoons mustard powder
2 tablespoons plain (all-purpose) flour
1 teaspoon salt
¼ teaspoon freshly ground black pepper
1 teaspoon brown sugar
1 x 1.5–2 kg (3–4 lb) rolled rib of beef
2 tablespoons olive oil
250 ml (8 fl oz) beer
chives, finely chopped, to serve

Serves 6

Preheat oven to 220°C (420°F). Mix together the mustard, flour, salt, pepper and brown sugar and rub all over meat, using a skewer to force some down into the centre of the joint.

Heat oil in a roasting pan, put meat in and place pan in the oven to sear the meat. Turn after 5 minutes. Pour beer over beef. Reduce heat to moderate (180°C/350°F) and roast for 1½–2 hours, basting occasionally.

Serve with vegetables. Brush vegetables with olive oil and bake in the oven for 25–30 minutes or until tender.

STEAK AND KIDNEY PIE

2 sheep's kidneys, skinned, halved and cored
1 teaspoon salt
freshly ground black pepper, to taste
2 tablespoons plain (all-purpose) flour
2 tablespoons butter
500 g (1 lb) casserole steak (chuck, blade, flank, skirt or
    round), trimmed and cut into 1 cm (½ in) cubes
125 ml (4 fl oz) water
375 g (12 oz) flaky pastry or puff pastry
2 tablespoons parsley, chopped
1 egg, beaten

Serves 4

Cut kidney into small pieces. Season flour with salt and pepper, then coat meat and kidneys with flour.

Melt butter in a heavy saucepan (use one that has a lid) over a moderate heat and brown steak and kidney, stirring continuously. Add water, cover tightly and simmer gently for 1 hour. Stir in parsley, then leave to cool.

Roll out pastry to a circle that is 2.5 cm (1 in) larger than the top of your pie dish. Cut a strip 1 cm (½ in) wide off the edge and place it on dampened rim of dish. Brush it with cold water. Spoon steak and kidney into dish. Place remaining pastry on top of mixture and press edges of pastry onto pastry rim to seal. Trim off excess pastry and decorate edge by flaking and fluting with the back of a fork. Glaze pie with egg and cut a cross on top about 2 cm deep.

Bake in the oven for 20 minutes, then reduce heat to moderately slow (165°C/325°F) and bake for a further 20 minutes.

T-BONE STEAK

4 t-bone steaks
olive oil
8 large mushrooms, whole
4 medium tomatoes, halved
salt and freshly ground black pepper, to taste

Serves 4

Allow steaks to stand at room temperature for 30 minutes before cooking. Cut fat around edge in two or three places to prevent steak curling.

Preheat grill until hot. Place steaks on grill rack and brush lean surface of meat lightly with oil. Grill steaks for 2 minutes on either side to seal surface of meat, turning with tongs or two spoons to avoid piercing the meat and letting the juices escape. Reduce heat and grill for a further 4–5 minutes on each side.

Place mushrooms on grill rack and cook for 2 minutes, then add tomatoes and grill for a further 3 minutes. Turn mushrooms and tomatoes once during grilling time. Season steak, mushrooms and tomatoes with salt and pepper before serving.

Serve with a tossed green salad and some flavored butter.

SWEET AND SOUR PORK

500 g (1 lb) pork fillets (pork chops can be used),
   cut into thin strips
3 tablespoons cornflour or plain (all-purpose) flour
olive oil for frying

SWEET AND SOUR SAUCE
250 ml (8 fl oz) chicken stock (see page 377)
125 ml (4 fl oz) pineapple juice
2 tablespoons vinegar
210 g (7 oz) canned pineapple (shredded or cubed)
1 carrot, finely sliced
1 cup green capsicum (bell pepper), sliced
salt and freshly ground black pepper, to taste
2 tablespoons cornflour
6 shallots, finely chopped
2 teaspoons soy sauce

Serves 6

Coat pork with cornflour. Heat oil in a frying pan and fry meat
for 20 minutes, or until golden brown and thoroughly cooked.
Drain meat well and keep hot.

To make sauce, place stock, pineapple juice, vinegar, pineapple,
carrot, celery, salt and pepper into a saucepan. Bring to the boil,
then reduce heat and simmer for 10 minutes, or until vegetables are
cooked, but firm.

In a cup, blend cornflour to a paste with a little water and add to
pineapple mixture. Boil for 2 minutes, or until thickened to desired
consistency. Just before serving, add shallots, soy sauce and pork
and stir to combine.

Serve on a bed of steamed rice.

VEAL WITH MOZZARELLA

750 g (1½ lb) veal steak, thinly sliced
seasoned flour (see glossary)
1 egg, beaten with 60 ml (2 fl oz) water
90 g (3 oz) fine breadcrumbs
    mixed with 30 g (1 oz) Parmesan cheese, grated
olive oil, for frying
2 tablespoons extra olive oil
2 cloves garlic, crushed
1 onion, finely chopped
1 x 470 g (15 oz) can tomatoes, peeled
3 tablespoons tomato paste
¼ teaspoon dried thyme
½ teaspoon caster (superfine) sugar
salt and freshly ground black pepper, to taste
250 g (8 oz) mozzarella cheese, thinly sliced

Serves 4

Preheat oven to 180°C (350°F). Flatten veal slices lightly, using the side of a meat mallet. Dip in seasoned flour, then in combined egg and water, and then coat with combined breadcrumbs and Parmesan cheese. Press crumbs on firmly.

Heat oil in a frying pan and fry veal until golden brown on both sides. Drain on absorbent paper.

Heat extra oil in a saucepan, then add garlic and onion and sauté for 5 minutes. Add tomatoes, tomato paste, thyme, sugar and salt and pepper. Cover, and simmer for 10 minutes.

Pour one-third of tomato mixture into an ovenproof casserole dish. Arrange veal on top, cover with cheese and pour over remaining sauce. Cook, uncovered, in the oven for 30–35 minutes.

Serve with a tossed green salad.

VEAL CORDON BLEU

8 medium-sized veal steaks, cut from leg
4 thin slices ham (about size of steaks)
4 thin slices Gruyère cheese
seasoned flour, for coating
1 egg, beaten with 1 tablespoon water
breadcrumbs, for coating
oil, for frying
lemon wedges, to garnish

Serves 4

Flatten veal steaks between two sheets of plastic cling wrap by beating with the side of a meat mallet or a rolling pin. Put the steaks in pairs, so that pieces in a pair are of a similar size. Place a slice of ham and a slice of cheese between each pair of steaks, keeping ham and cheese 5 mm (¼ in) in from edge of veal all round. Beat edges to seal. Coat veal with seasoned flour, dip carefully in egg, then coat with breadcrumbs, pressing them on firmly.

Allow to stand for 10 minutes, then heat oil in a frying pan and shallow fry veal over a moderate heat until light golden brown. Turn carefully and brown other side. It will take about 5 minutes to completely cook the veal. Drain on absorbent paper and serve piping hot.

Garnish with lemon wedges and serve with boiled new potatoes and vegetables.

Note: If cheese leaks out of the steak and causes spitting, place a slice of potato in the pan – it will absorb moisture.

VIENNA SCHNITZEL

500 g (1 lb) thinly cut veal steak, cut from leg
1 clove garlic, crushed (optional)
1 tablespoon lemon juice
salt and freshly ground black pepper, to taste
plain (all-purpose) flour, for coating
1 egg, beaten with 1 tablespoon water
breadcrumbs, for coating
olive oil, for frying
hard-boiled egg, anchovy fillets, capers, lemon slices
    and parsley, to garnish

Serves 4

Flatten veal between two pieces of plastic cling wrap, using the side
of a meat mallet or rolling pin. Cut skin on edges to prevent curling
during cooking. Lay veal on a plate and set aside.

Mix garlic (optional) with lemon juice and brush onto veal.
Season with salt and pepper and allow to stand for 30 minutes.
Dip each slice of veal into flour, then egg, and finally breadcrumbs,
pressing them firmly on to coat veal completely. Refrigerate for
1 hour.

Heat oil in a frying pan and shallow fry veal steaks over a
moderate heat for about 2 minutes on either side, or until golden
brown. Lift veal onto absorbent paper to drain, then place on a hot
serving platter.

Garnish each schnitzel with a slice of hard-boiled egg and top
with a rolled anchovy fillet, a few capers, lemon slice and parsley.

Serve with boiled new potatoes, sauerkraut and a tossed salad.

SWEETS & DESSERTS

APPLE CRUMBLE

6 cooking apples, peeled, cored and sliced
3 cloves
125 ml (4 fl oz) honey
125 g (4 oz) plain (all-purpose) wholemeal flour
100 g (3½ oz) oatmeal
30 g (1 oz) wheat germ
¼ teaspoon salt
90 g (3 oz) raw sugar
185 g (6 oz) butter
whipped cream or vanilla custard sauce
    (see page 373), for serving

Serves 8

Preheat oven to 200°C (400°F). Place apples in an ovenproof dish.
Add cloves and pour over honey.
    Place flour, oatmeal, wheat germ, salt and sugar in a bowl.
Rub in butter until mixture is crumbly, then spread mixture
over apples.
    Bake in the oven for 1 hour, or until top is golden brown.
Serve with vanilla custard sauce.

BAKED APPLES

8 prunes, stoned and chopped
2 tablespoons raisins
4 cooking apples, cored
4 tablespoons honey
30 g (1 oz) butter
4 tablespoons water
vanilla custard sauce (see page 373), for serving

Serves 8

Preheat oven to 180°C (350°F). In a bowl, combine prunes with raisins. Stuff apples with prunes and raisins and place in a baking dish. Pour honey over apples and dot with butter. Add water to baking dish.

Bake in the oven for ¾–1 hour, or until apples are tender. Serve hot with vanilla custard sauce.

BAKED CUSTARD

2 large eggs
60 g (2 oz) caster (superfine) sugar
500 ml (1 pint) milk, scalded
1 teaspoon vanilla
$\frac{1}{8}$ teaspoon salt
1 teaspoon nutmeg, grated

Serves 4–6

Preheat oven to 180°C (350°F). In a bowl, beat eggs lightly.
Add sugar and combine, then add scalded milk, slowly, until
sugar is dissolved. Add vanilla and stir through, then add salt and
stir through.

Pour into a large pie dish or ovenproof dish. Sprinkle a little
grated nutmeg on top, set in a shallow tin or dish half full of water
and bake in the oven for 20–30 minutes, or until a knife piercing the
custard comes out clean.

Serve hot or cold.

BREAD AND BUTTER PUDDING

CUSTARD
2 eggs
1 tablespoon caster (superfine) sugar
150 ml (5 fl oz) milk, warmed
pinch of nutmeg, grated
2 large or 4 small slices of bread
butter
60 g (2 oz) dried fruit
extra sugar

Serves 4

To make custard, beat eggs in a bowl with a fork. Beat in sugar and milk; the milk must not boil, or it will curdle the eggs. Pour into a greased pie dish or basin and top with grated nutmeg. Put the basin into a steamer over very hot water and cook steadily for about 1½ hours. Make sure that the water does not boil – this will curdle the custard.

Preheat oven to 180°C (350°F). Remove crusts from bread, and butter bread thinly. Cut into neat squares or triangles and arrange in a pie dish. Add dried fruit and pour egg custard over the top. Allow to stand for 30 minutes. Sprinkle the top with a little sugar and bake for 1 hour in the oven. If the pudding appears to be cooking too quickly after 45 minutes, reduce to 130°C (265°F).

BANANA CAKE

125 g (4 oz) butter
125 g (4 oz) caster sugar
1 teaspoon vanilla
2 small eggs
3 small ripe bananas, mashed
250 g (8 oz) self-raising flour, sifted
1 teaspoon bicarbonate of soda (baking soda)
1 tablespoon milk
250 ml (8 fl oz) fresh cream, whipped

FROSTING
30 g (1 oz) cream cheese
30 g (1 oz) butter
100 g (3½ oz) icing sugar
1 teaspoon lemon juice

Serves 6–8

Preheat oven to 200°C (400°F). In a bowl, cream butter, caster sugar and vanilla thoroughly. Add eggs, one at a time, beating well after each addition. Add bananas to mixture and combine well. Add half flour and fold in lightly.

Dissolve bicarbonate of soda in milk and add to mixture. Stir in gently. Add remaining flour and mix well.

Pour mixture into two greased and floured 20 cm (8 in) cake tins and bake in the oven for about 25 minutes. The cake is ready when a wooden skewer inserted into the centre comes out clean.

When cold, join cakes with cream, ice with lemon frosting.

BANANA CAKE

125 g (4 oz) butter
125 g (4 oz) caster sugar
1 teaspoon vanilla
2 small eggs
3 small ripe bananas, mashed
250 g (8 oz) self-raising flour, sifted
1 teaspoon bicarbonate of soda (baking soda)
1 tablespoon milk
250 ml (8 fl oz) fresh cream, whipped

FROSTING
30 g (1 oz) cream cheese
30 g (1 oz) butter
100 g (3½ oz) icing sugar
1 teaspoon lemon juice

Serves 6–8

Preheat oven to 200°C (400°F). In a bowl, cream butter, caster sugar and vanilla thoroughly. Add eggs, one at a time, beating well after each addition. Add bananas to mixture and combine well. Add half flour and fold in lightly.

Dissolve bicarbonate of soda in milk and add to mixture. Stir in gently. Add remaining flour and mix well.

Pour mixture into two greased and floured 20 cm (8 in) cake tins and bake in the oven for about 25 minutes. The cake is ready when a wooden skewer inserted into the centre comes out clean.

When cold, join cakes with cream, ice with lemon frosting.

CARROT CAKE

125 g (4 oz) self-raising flour
180 g (6 oz) brown sugar, packed tightly
2 teaspoons cinnamon
100 g (3 oz) carrot, finely grated
75 g (2 ½ oz) raisins, chopped
2 eggs
125 ml (4 fl oz) olive oil
¼ cup walnuts, chopped

FROSTING
30 g (1 oz) cream cheese
30 g (1 oz) butter
100 g (3½ oz) icing sugar
1 teaspoon lemon juice

Serves 6–8

In a bowl, mix together flour, sugar, cinnamon, carrots and raisins.
Add eggs and oil and combine thoroughly. Pour into a 20 cm (8 in)
microwave safe cake tin lined with greaseproof paper and cook
medium–high for 8 minutes until just cooked. Let cake stand for
5 minutes.

To make frosting, beat cream cheese and butter in a bowl until
smooth; for best results, use an electric mixer. Gradually mix in
icing sugar and lemon juice.

Allow cake to cool then top with frosting and walnuts.

Note: This is a microwave recipe.

CHEESECAKE

CRUST
1 x 225 g (7 oz) packet plain sweet biscuits
125 g (4 oz) butter

FILLING
250 g (8 oz) cream cheese
80 ml (3 fl oz) lemon juice
1 x 410 g (13½ oz) can condensed milk
whipped cream, to garnish
berries to garnish

Serves 10

To make the crust, put biscuits in a plastic bag and seal the top with an elastic band or twist tie. Using a rolling pin, crush the biscuits in the bag – you will need to roll again and again. Pour biscuit crumbs into a bowl.

Melt butter in a saucepan over medium heat, then pour melted butter over biscuit crumbs and mix thoroughly. Tip biscuit mixture into a spring-form cake tin and spread it out, then press it down firmly with the back of a spoon. Make sure you press some up the sides as well. The biscuit crust should be about 5 mm (¼ in) thick all over. Put the cake tin in the refrigerator for 20 minutes while you prepare the filling.

To make the filling, put the cream cheese in a bowl and mash it up with a fork. Add lemon juice and condensed milk and beat with an egg beater until the mixture is smooth. Pour cheese mixture into the pie dish and smooth over gently with a spoon. Put the cheesecake in the refrigerator and leave to set for at least 4 hours.

When ready to serve, garnish with whipped cream and berries.

CHOC-COFFEE SURPRISES

125 g (4 oz) butter
180 g (6 oz) icing (confectioners') sugar
1 teaspoon vanilla
1 teaspoon hot water
2 teaspoons instant coffee powder
60 g (2 oz) caster (superfine) sugar
80 ml (3 fl oz) water
140 g (4½ oz) desiccated coconut
2 teaspoons vanilla
1 egg white, lightly beaten
125 g (4 oz) dark chocolate, chopped
30 g (1 oz) copha, melted

Makes 25

In a bowl, cream butter, icing sugar and vanilla until light and fluffy. In a cup, combine hot water and instant coffee. Add this to butter and sugar mixture and beat well. Refrigerate until firm.

Roll teaspoonfuls of mixture into small balls and chill for 30 minutes.

In a saucepan, stir sugar and water over a medium heat until sugar dissolves. Bring to the boil, remove from heat and stir in coconut, vanilla and egg white. Keep stirring until well combined, then set aside to cool.

Mold about two teaspoonfuls of the coconut mixture around each coffee ball and chill.

Melt chocolate and copha together in a basin over a saucepan of hot water or in the top of a double boiler. Dip chilled balls into chocolate and copha mixture. Refrigerate for 24 hours before eating, to allow flavor to develop.

CHOCOLATE AND DATE SLICE

180 g (6 oz) dates, chopped
125 g (4 oz) self-raising (self-rising) flour
250 g (8 oz) brown sugar
45 g (1½ oz) desiccated coconut
90 g (3 oz) cup chocolate bits
125 g (4 oz) butter
1 tablespoon golden syrup
1 egg, beaten

Serves 6–8

Preheat oven to 180°C (350°F). In a bowl, combine all the
dry ingredients.

In a small saucepan, melt butter and stir in golden syrup.
Cool slightly then add egg and mix. Add the melted butter mixture to
the dry ingredients and mix together well.

Line a rectangular cake pan (about 30 x 20 cm/ 12 x 10 in) with
baking paper (or just grease the dish) and pour mixture in. Press it
flat with the back of a spoon. Bake in the oven for 20–25 minutes,
or until golden brown.

Variation: Add mixed fruit and/or mixed nuts instead of all the
dates, and/or ice the slice with lemon frosting (see page 350) when
it has cooled.

CHOCOLATE FUDGE

750 g (1 ²/₃ lbs) caster (superfine) sugar
1½ tablespoons cocoa
250 ml (8 fl oz) milk
1 tablespoon glucose syrup
20 g (²/₃ oz) butter
few drops vanilla essence

Makes 36 squares

Combine sugar, cocoa, milk and glucose syrup in a saucepan.
Stir over a low heat until sugar is dissolved and begins to boil.
Watch that it does not boil over. Continue cooking until a small
amount of the fudge forms a soft ball when dropped into a glass of
cold water (about 10 minutes).

Remove fudge from the heat and tip it into a large bowl.
Add butter and vanilla essence and beat until the mixture is thick
and creamy. Pour immediately into a greased cake tin (4.5 cm x
3 cm/11 x 7 in) and cut into small squares.

Put the fudge in the refrigerator until it is cold, then break it
into squares.

CHOCOLATE LOG

60 ml (2 fl oz) milk
625 ml (1 ¼ pints) fresh cream
6 teaspoons caster (superfine) sugar
225 g (7 oz) plain chocolate biscuits

Serves 6

Pour milk in one bowl and 315 ml (11 oz) cream in another.
Add 3 teaspoons sugar to cream and whip it with an egg beater
until stiff.

Dip one biscuit quickly in the milk and cover one side of it with
whipped cream. Stand the biscuit on its edge in a long narrow
loaf tin. Dip the next biscuit in the milk, cover one side with cream
and stand it right next to the first biscuit. Continue in this way
along the plate, forming a log and using all the biscuits and all the
whipped cream.

Put the remaining cream and sugar in the bowl and beat until
thick. Spread this cream all over the log, covering it completely.
Decorate with chocolate buttons or nuts as you wish.

Put the log in the refrigerator and leave for at least 4 hours.
It tastes better if you eat it the next day. To serve the log, cut it
diagonally so that each piece is striped.

CHOCOLATE PUDDING

60 g (2 oz) self-raising (self-rising) flour
2 tablespoons cocoa
60 g (2 oz) breadcrumbs
60 g (2 oz) butter
60 g (2 oz) caster (superfine) sugar
1 egg (optional)
dash of milk
few drops vanilla essence

Serves 4

Sift flour and cocoa into a bowl, then add all other dry ingredients and mix thoroughly. In another bowl, beat egg (if using) and milk, then stir in vanilla essence.

Stir enough liquid into the dry mixture to give it a slightly sticky consistency. Grease and flour a bowl and put the mixture in it. Cover with greased greaseproof paper and steam or boil for about 1¾ hours.

Serve with vanilla custard sauce (see page 314).

STRAWBERRY SHORTCAKE

125 g (4 oz) butter
125 g (4 oz) caster (superfine) sugar
1 egg
1 teaspoon vanilla essence
180 g (6 oz) plain (all-purpose) flour
30 g (1 oz) cornflour (cornstarch)
2 teaspoons baking powder
2 tablespoons milk
2 punnets strawberries, crushed leaving some whole,
    to garnish
250 ml (8 fl oz) fresh cream, whipped

Serves 6–8

Preheat oven to 180°C (350°F). In a bowl, cream butter and sugar
together until light and fluffy. Add egg and vanilla and beat well.

In another bowl, sift dry ingredients. Add to butter and sugar
mixture a little at a time, alternately with milk.

Pour mixture to a greased 20 cm (8 in) spring-form cake tin and
bake in the oven for 30–35 minutes, until a skewer inserted into the
middle of the cake comes out clean.

Remove cake from tin and allow to stand until quite cold, then
cut it horizontally, through the centre. Cover the lower half with
whipped cream and crushed strawberries in separate layers.
Place the other half on top and cover it with whipped cream and the
choicest berries, either whole or halved, placing the cut side down
on cream.

CHOCOLATE MOUSSE

2 tablespoons brandy
5 eggs, separated
375 g (12 oz) good quality dark chocolate, chopped
300 ml (10 fl oz) thickened cream

Serves 8

In a small saucepan, beat brandy and egg yolks until smooth. Meanwhile, melt chocolate in a bowl over hot water, stirring until smooth. Cool chocolate, then whisk in the yolk mixture.

In another bowl, beat egg whites until they form soft peaks. In a third bowl, beat cream until stiff. Fold egg whites and cream into chocolate mixture until no streaks remain.

Spoon into 8 mousse pots or 1 large serving dish. Cover and chill for at least 3 hours, or until set.

CHOCOLATE STRAWBERRIES

125 g (4 oz) dark chocolate, chopped
125 g (4 oz) white chocolate, chopped
60 g (2 oz) copha
500 g (1 lb) strawberries, washed

Serves 8

Melt the dark chocolate and half of the copha gently in a bowl over hot water, or in the top of a double boiler, then cool slightly.

Melt the white chocolate and rest of the copha gently in a bowl over hot water, or in the top of a double boiler, then cool slightly.

Hold each berry by the stem and dip it (to two-thirds of its depth) into either the dark or white chocolate mixture. Place dipped berries on a plastic-covered tray. Chill. Serve with coffee.

Note: Chocolate strawberries can be made (and kept in the refrigerator) for up to 24 hours before serving.

CHOCOLATE WALNUT BROWNIES

60 g (2 oz) plain (all-purpose) flour
1 tablespoon bran
¼ teaspoon baking powder
60 g (2 oz) walnuts, chopped
60 g (2 oz) butter
60 g (2 oz) cooking chocolate
180 g (6 oz) brown sugar
2 eggs, beaten
½ teaspoon vanilla essence

Makes 16 squares

Preheat oven to 180°C (350°F). Grease a 28 x 18 cm (11 x 7 in) shallow baking tin. Cut a piece of greaseproof paper long enough to cover the sides of the tin, going a little higher than the edge of the tin. Press greaseproof paper inside the tin, cutting down into each corner so you can fold the paper round to fit.

In a bowl, mix together flour, bran, baking powder and walnuts.

In a saucepan, melt butter with chocolate and sugar. Cool slightly, then whisk in eggs and vanilla essence with a fork. Pour this into the flour mixture and mix well.

Pour mixture into the prepared tin and bake in the oven for 35 minutes, until the cake has risen and the centre springs back when lightly pressed. Leave to cool in the tin, then cut into squares.

COCONUT MACAROONS

2 egg whites
150 g (5 oz) caster (superfine) sugar
½ teaspoon cornflour
125 g (4 oz) desiccated coconut
vanilla or almond essence

Makes 30

Preheat oven to 130°C (265°F). In a bowl, beat egg whites until
they are stiff. Gradually add caster sugar, beating well after each
addition. Add cornflour and fold in well.

Place mixture in an enamel, stainless steel or other heatproof
bowl and beat over a saucepan of boiling water until mixture begins
to cook on the bottom of the basin. Fold in the coconut and vanilla
or almond essence.

Place teaspoons of the mixture onto a greased baking tray and
bake in the oven for 25 minutes.

COFFEE CAKE

125 g (4 oz) butter
185 g (6 oz) caster (superfine) sugar
1 egg
½ teaspoon vanilla essence
250 g (8 oz) self-raising flour
½ teaspoon salt
185 ml (6 fl oz) milk
2 tablespoons golden syrup
1 teaspoon ground cinnamon
¼ teaspoon ground nutmeg
¼ teaspoon ground cloves
½ teaspoon ground cinnamon

TOPPING
125 g (4 oz) brown sugar
60–90 g (2–3 oz) chopped walnuts
2 good tablespoons plain (all-purpose) flour
½ teaspoon ground cinnamon
60 g (2 oz) butter, melted

Makes 12–16 squares

Preheat oven to 180°C (350°F). Cream butter and sugar in a bowl until light and fluffy. Add egg and beat well, then add vanilla essence. Sift the flour and salt together, then add to the creamed mixture alternately with the milk, a little at a time and stir until well combined. Divide mixture in half.

To one half add golden syrup and spices. Line a 23 cm (9 in) square cake tin with baking paper, and spoon mixtures alternately into the cake tin. Zigzag a spatula through the mixture to give a marbled effect.

To make topping, put brown sugar, walnuts, flour and cinnamon into a bowl, then add butter and mix well. Sprinkle mixture over dough in cake tin and bake in the oven for 30 minutes. Let cake cool, then cut into squares.

COFFEE SLICE

125 g (4 oz) butter
125 g (4 oz) self-raising (self-rising) flour
75 g (2½ oz) desiccated coconut
250 g (8 oz) brown sugar

TOPPING
25 g (¾ oz) butter
2 tablespoons instant coffee
435 ml (14½ fl oz) condensed milk
2 tablespoons golden syrup
50 g (1½ oz) chopped walnuts

Makes 24 squares

Preheat oven to 180°C (350°F). Grease the inside of a slice cake tin (4.5 cm x 3 cm/11 x 7 in).

Melt butter in a saucepan over a low heat. Place flour, coconut and brown sugar into a bowl. Pour melted butter over dry ingredients and mix together. Put the mixture into the tin and press it down all over with the back of a spoon. Bake on the centre shelf of the oven for 20 minutes.

To make the topping, put butter and coffee in a saucepan and melt over a low heat. Add condensed milk and golden syrup and stir over a low heat until thoroughly combined. Add the chopped walnuts and stir through when mixture has cooled. Pour the coffee topping over the cooked base.

CRÊPES

315 ml (1¼ cups) pancake batter (see page 326)
butter, for cooking

Serves 4–6

Heat a frying pan on low, and add enough butter to cover the
bottom liberally. As the pan heats, tilt it to allow butter to run
all over the surface. Drain off extra butter, leaving just a film in
the pan.

Off the heat, pour in enough batter to run all over pan bottom –
about 1 tablespoon for a pan 15 cm (6 in) across. Replace pan over
heat and cook until the upper surface of the crepe appears bubbly.
Run a small spatula around the edge to loosen the crepe, then slide
the knife under and turn or toss crepe over. The side cooked first is
served as the outer side.

Turn finished crepes on to a wire rack and cover with a clean tea
towel. Stack slightly overlapping and wrap to keep warm.

Serve with jam and freshly whipped cream or lemon juice
and sugar.

PANCAKES WITH MAPLE SYRUP

125 g (4 oz) self-raising (self-rising) flour
pinch of salt
½ teaspoon bicarbonate of soda (baking soda)
250 ml (8 fl oz) milk
3 tablespoons caster (superfine) sugar
1 egg
butter, for pan
bottle of maple syrup

Makes 8

Place flour, salt, bicarbonate of soda, milk, sugar and egg in a jug and beat together until there are no lumps.

Melt a small piece of butter in a frying pan over a medium heat. Pour a little pancake mixture into the centre of the pan – the mixture should spread out to about 15 cm (6 in) across. Cook until the bubbles on top have burst, then flip the pancake over using a spatula. Cook for another minute or two, till underside is golden brown, then lift the pancake onto a plate. Repeat until all mixture is used.

As pancakes are cooked, stack them on a plate, cover with aluminum foil and put in a very slow oven (100°C/200°F) to keep warm. Serve with maple syrup.

Variation: Serve with lemon and sugar or fresh berries instead of maple syrup.

DATE SLICE

125 g (4 oz) self-raising (self-rising) flour
60 g (2 oz) desiccated coconut
60 g (2 oz) caster (superfine) sugar
150 g (5 oz) dates, chopped
125 g (4 oz) butter
lemon frosting (see page 350)

Makes 24 squares

Preheat oven to 180°C (350°F). Sift flour into a bowl and mix in coconut, sugar and dates. Melt butter in a saucepan over a low heat. Add melted butter to dry mixture and mix thoroughly with a wooden spoon. Put mixture into a greased slice tin and press down firmly with the back of a spoon. Place slice on the centre shelf of the oven and bake for 25 minutes.

Remove slice from oven and cover with lemon frosting while it is still hot. Cut into squares while it is still warm, but leave it in the tin to cool.

CUSTARD

60 g (2 oz) caster (superfine) sugar
1 tablespoon cornflour (cornstarch)
2 egg yolks
500 ml (1 pint) milk
piece of lemon rind, finely peeled
vanilla essence (optional)

Serves 4–6

Mix sugar, cornflour and egg yolks in a small saucepan with enough of the milk to make a paste, then add remaining milk and lemon rind. Bring just to the boil, stirring continuously until thickened.

Remove from heat. Add a little vanilla essence, to taste (if using). Pour custard into serving jug or bowl. Cover the top of the jug or bowl with a piece of greaseproof paper or plastic cling wrap and chill until serving time.

PIKELETS

1 egg
125 g (4 oz) self-raising (self-rising) flour, sifted
pinch of salt
¼ teaspoon bicarbonate of soda (baking soda)
165 ml (5 ½ fl oz) milk
1 teaspoon vinegar
3 tablespoons caster (superfine) sugar
2 tablespoons butter

Serves 6

In a bowl, beat egg, then add flour, salt, bicarbonate of soda, milk, vinegar and sugar. Mix until smooth.

Melt butter in a frying pan and pour mixture in a tablespoon at a time to cook. When you see bubbles forming at the side of the pikelet, flip the pikelet and cook it for another minute. Continue until you have used all the mixture.

FAIRY CAKES

125 g (4 oz) butter
150 g (5 oz) caster (superfine) sugar
2 eggs
250 g (8 oz) self-raising flour, sifted
125 ml (4 fl oz) milk

Makes 25 cakes

Preheat oven to 190°C (375°F). Place butter and sugar into a large bowl and beat together with a wooden spoon until creamy. Beat eggs (one at a time) into butter and sugar. Slowly stir in flour and milk. Stir to remove any lumps.

If using a muffin tin, grease each hollow and sprinkle lightly with flour. If using paper patty cases, place them side by side on a flat tray. Place a heaped teaspoonful of the cake mixture into each patty case. Place the tray in the centre of the oven and bake for 15 minutes.

When the cakes are cool, you can ice them and cover them with sprinkles or make them into butterfly cakes (see page 336).

FRUIT CRUMBLE

500 g (1 lb) stewed or canned fruit

TOPPING
125 g (4 oz) plain (all-purpose) flour
50 g (1²⁄₃ oz) hard butter
75 g (2½ oz) caster (superfine) sugar

Serves 6

Preheat oven to 180°C (350°F). If using canned fruit, drain off all the juice. Place fruit in a 20 cm (8 in) ovenproof dish.

Sift flour into a bowl. Grate the butter over the flour and mix through with a knife. Sprinkle sugar over flour and butter and mix again with a wooden spoon. Sprinkle crumble mixture over fruit and press down lightly with a spoon. Put the fruit crumble on the centre shelf of the oven. Bake for 35 minutes, or until the top is golden brown.

GRANDMA'S CHRISTMAS CAKE

250 g (8 oz) dates
250 g (8 oz) raisins
220 g (7 oz) currants
220 g (7 oz) dried pineapple
220 g (7 oz) dried figs
750 ml (1.5 pints) water
180 g (6 oz) wholemeal flour
375 (12 oz) self-raising (self-raising) flour, sifted
180 ml (6 fl oz) olive oil

Serves 16–20

Chop all fruit and soak in water for 1 hour. Drain off water, reserving 125 ml (½ cup) of the liquid.

Preheat oven to 130°C (265°F). In a bowl, mix flour, reserved water and oil to a soft dough. Add soaked fruit and mix thoroughly. Spread mixture into a greased 25 cm (10 in) square cake tin and cover with foil. Bake in the oven for 3½ hours, removing the foil after 3 hours of cooking. The cake is ready when a wooden skewer inserted into the middle of the cake comes out clean.

LEMON MERINGUE PIE

185 g (6 oz) short crust pastry (see page 347)

FILLING
3 dessertspoons cornflour (cornstarch)
   or custard powder
315 ml (10 ½ fl oz) water
60 g (2 oz) margarine
90–120 g (3–4 oz) caster (superfine) sugar
2 egg yolks
2 lemons

MERINGUE
2 egg whites
60 g (2 oz) caster (superfine) sugar

Serves 4

Preheat oven to 220°C (420°F). Line a pie dish with the pastry and bake blind for 20–25 minutes. Reduce oven temperature to 120°C (250°F).

To make the filling, blend cornflour with cold water in a saucepan. Cook gently until thickened. Add margarine, sugar and egg yolks. Finely grate zest of lemons, then juice lemons. Stir zest and juice into mixture. Pour into the pastry case.

In a bowl, whisk egg whites until they are stiff, then fold in nearly all the sugar. Pile on top of the lemon filling and dust with the remaining sugar. Bake for 45 minutes in the oven at the lower temperature, until the meringue feels firm to the touch. If you bake the meringue more quickly, it will not stay crisp when cold.

PATTY CAKES

90 g (3 oz) butter
90 g (3 oz) caster (superfine) sugar
½ teaspoon vanilla essence
2 eggs
180 g (6 oz) self-raising (self-rising) flour
pinch of salt
2 tablespoons milk

Makes 20 medium-sized patties

Preheat oven to 220°C (420°F). In a bowl, beat together butter, sugar and vanilla essence until mixture is light and fluffy. Add eggs one at a time, beating well after each addition.

In another bowl, sift flour and salt together. Add to butter and sugar mixture, a little at a time, alternately with milk. Mix well after each addition.

Spoon mixture into greased patty tins or patty cases. Bake in the oven for 12–15 minutes.

Allow cakes to cool, then decorate them with warm icing, or make them into butterfly cakes or baskets.

For butterfly cakes, cut a slice (1–1.5 cm/½ in) off the top of each cake, then place a spoonful of cream on the cake, then cut the top in half and place the pieces on the cream at an angle, to represent the wings of butterflies.

PEANUT BRITTLE CRUMBLE

6 cooking apples, peeled and sliced
2 tablespoons lemon juice
½ teaspoon lemon rind, grated
60 g (2 oz) butter
60 g (2 oz) flour
125 g (4 oz) brown sugar
¼ cup smooth peanut butter

Serves 6–8

Preheat oven to 180°C (350°F). Place apples in a 20 cm (8 in) pie dish and sprinkle with lemon juice and rind.

In a bowl, rub butter into flour with your fingertips, until mixture is crumbly. Add sugar and mix well. Using two knives, add peanut butter.

Sprinkle crumb mixture over apples and bake in the oven for 30–40 minutes, or until apples are tender.

Serve warm, topped with vanilla custard sauce (see page 373), whipped cream or ice cream.

RAISIN OATMEAL MUFFINS

125 g (4 oz) plain (all-purpose) flour
3 teaspoons baking powder
¼ teaspoon salt
60 g (2 oz) butter
100 g (3½ oz) rolled oats
125 g (4 oz) brown sugar, firmly packed
125 g (4 oz) raisins
250 ml (8 fl oz) milk
1 egg, beaten
2 tablespoons caster (superfine) sugar
½ teaspoon cinnamon

Makes 24

Preheat oven to 200°C (400°F). Sift flour, baking powder and salt together into a bowl, then rub in butter with your fingertips, until mixture resembles fine breadcrumbs. Add rolled oats, brown sugar, raisins, milk and egg, and mix well.

In a cup, combine sugar and cinnamon.

Pour mixture into deep, greased patty pans so that they are all three-quarters full, and sprinkle lightly with cinnamon sugar.

Bake in the oven for 18–20 minutes, or until a skewer inserted into the middle of the muffin comes out clean.

SHORTBREAD BISCUITS

125 g (4 oz) butter
60 g (2 oz) caster (superfine) sugar
1 teaspoon vanilla essence
100 g (3½ oz) plain (all-purpose) flour
60 g (2 oz) rice flour
25 g (¾ oz) cornflour (cornstarch)

Makes 16

Preheat oven to 200°C (400°F). In a bowl, cream butter and sugar, then add vanilla. While mixing, slowly add flours and form a dough.

Place mixture onto a baking tray covered with baking paper. Place tray in the freezer for 10 minutes (or the refrigerator for 20 minutes). Remove mixture from the freezer and cut into desired biscuit shape.

Cook in the oven for about 10 minutes, or until golden.

VANILLA CREAMED RICE PUDDING

1 tablespoon short grain rice
625 ml (1¼ pints) milk
1 dessertspoon caster (superfine) sugar
1 teaspoon butter
5 cm (2 in) vanilla pod, seeds removed
2 teaspoons ground nutmeg

Serves 6–8

Preheat oven to 155°C (310°F). Stir rice, milk and sugar together in a buttered ovenproof dish. Add vanilla seeds. Sprinkle top with nutmeg. Place on middle shelf of the oven and cook for 2–2½ hours. Stir the pudding gently once or twice during cooking, slipping a spoon under the skin to do so.

Serve hot or cold. When serving cold, remove the skin and sprinkle top with sugar and more nutmeg.

YORKSHIRE PUDDING

250 g (8 oz) plain (all-purpose) flour
pinch of salt
1 egg
315 ml (10½ fl oz) milk

Serves 4–6

Preheat oven to 250°C (485°F). Sift flour and salt together into a
bowl. Make a well in the centre and drop egg in. Add half the milk,
a little at a time, and gradually stir in the flour from the sides of the
bowl, using a wooden spoon. Mix until smooth, then beat batter
with the back of the spoon for 5–10 minutes. When thoroughly
beaten, air bubbles appear on the surface. Cover batter and allow to
stand for 30 minutes.

   Stir in remaining milk, to give a thin batter, just before cooking.
Grease muffin pans or a shallow square 17.5 cm (9 in) cake tin
and place in the oven until oil is smoking hot. Remove muffin pans
and quickly pour in batter so that it comes halfway up each pan.
Return to the oven and cook until yorkshire pudding is crisp, puffed
up and golden brown. Serve at once.

BASICS

DIPS

FRENCH ONION DIP

1 packet French onion soup
300 g (10 oz) sour cream
1 teaspoon Tabasco sauce (optional)

Serves 4

Mix all ingredients and serve.

LAYERED SEAFOOD CREAM CHEESE DIP

250 g (8 oz) cream cheese
125 g (4 oz) sour cream
60 ml (2 fl oz) mayonnaise
180 g (6 oz) cooked shrimp
125–180 ml (4-6 fl oz) seafood cocktail sauce
250 g (8 oz) mozzarella cheese, shredded
1 green capsicum (bell pepper),
    seeds and pith removed and diced
4 shallots (scallions), finely sliced
1 tomato, seeded and diced

Serves 8–10

In a bowl, combine cream cheese, sour cream and mayonnaise.
Spread mixture in a circle over the base of a serving platter.
Layer the remaining ingredients in order over the top. Chill for
1 hour before serving.
    Serve with corn chips or savory biscuits.

DOUGH AND PASTRY

BASIC SCONE DOUGH

250 g (8 oz) plain (all-purpose) flour
2½ tablespoons baking powder
½ teaspoon salt
60 g (2 oz) butter
185 ml (6 fl oz) milk

Makes 12 scones

Sift flour, baking powder and salt into a bowl. Cut butter into flour in small pieces and rub in lightly with your fingertips, until mixture resembles very fine breadcrumbs. Make a well in the centre of the flour, pour in milk and mix to a soft dough. Turn dough onto a lightly floured board and knead very lightly until smooth. Roll out to 1 cm (½ in) thickness and use as required. Dough will keep in the refrigerator for 3–4 days.

To cook, place scones close together on a baking tray and cook in the oven at 200°C (450°F) for 10–15 minutes.

BATTER

60 g (2 oz) self-raising (self-rising) flour
15 g (½ oz) butter, melted
125 ml (4 fl oz) lukewarm water
1 egg white
¼ teaspoon salt

Serves 2

Sift flour into a bowl. Make a well in the centre and add butter and water. Beat together until a smooth batter is formed. Let stand until ready to use. Batter will keep in the refrigerator for 5–7 days.

In another bowl, whisk egg white and salt together until stiff. Gently fold into batter and use immediately.

PASTA DOUGH

1 tablespoon salt
3 tablespoons olive oil
5 eggs
375 g (12 oz) plain (all-purpose) flour

Serves 4

Combine salt, olive oil, and eggs in food processor.

Gradually add flour, pulsing to mix. Use a pasta machine to thin out and cut the dough. Start with a small piece of dough and knead it down until fairly flat. Feed it through the machine at the #1 setting. It's thin enough to use when you can see your hand behind it. Cut the dough into desired pieces. Let dry on paper toweling. When dry run the dough through the machine to cut it.

SHORT CRUST PASTRY

250 g (8 oz) plain (all-purpose) flour
½ teaspoon salt
60 g (2 oz) butter
3–4 tablespoons cold water

Makes 300 g (10 oz)

Sift flour and salt into a bowl. Cut butter into flour in small
pieces and rub into flour lightly with your fingertips, until mixture
resembles fine breadcrumbs. Add cold water gradually and mix to a
stiff dough – the dough should leave the sides of the bowl cleanly.
Knead pastry lightly until smooth. Wrap pastry in plastic cling wrap
and chill for 30 minutes. Roll out and use as required.

This pastry will keep well in the refrigerator for 3–4 days.

ICING

CHOCOLATE FROSTING

250 g (8 oz) icing (confectioners') sugar
3 tablespoons cocoa
2 teaspoons butter
3 tablespoons hot water

Makes 260 g (8 oz)

Sift icing sugar and cocoa into a bowl. Put butter into a second bowl and pour over hot water. Stir to melt the butter. Pour butter and water over icing sugar and cocoa and stir until mixture is smooth. Add a little more cocoa to thicken the icing or warm water to thin it.

Variation:

Mocha Icing: Dissolve 1 teaspoon instant coffee in the butter and hot water and make the icing as above.

ORANGE OR LEMON FROSTING

250 g (8 oz) icing (confectioners') sugar
4 tablespoons orange juice or lemon juice

Makes 260 g (8 oz)

Sift icing sugar into a bowl and pour over juice. Stir until the icing is smooth.

PLAIN FROSTING

250 g (8 oz) icing (confectioners') sugar
2 teaspoons butter
2 tablespoons milk

Makes 260 g (8 oz)

Sift icing sugar into a bowl. Add butter and milk and mix until smooth. Color as desired.

WARM FROSTING AND VARIATIONS

125 g (4 oz) icing (confectioners') sugar, sifted
1 teaspoon butter
60 ml (2 fl oz) warm milk

Makes 185 g (6 oz)

Place icing sugar in a bowl and mix to a thick paste with melted butter and a little milk. Heat over boiling water until icing is liquid enough to be poured.

Variations:

- **Coffee frosting:** Add 1 teaspoon coffee essence.
- **Chocolate frosting:** Add 1 tablespoon cocoa.
- **Mocha frosting:** Add ½ teaspoon coffee essence and 1 dessertspoon cocoa.
- **Lemon frosting:** Use lemon juice instead of milk.
- **Orange frosting:** Use orange juice instead of milk.

SAUCES AND DRESSING

APPLE SAUCE

4 large cooking apples, peeled and sliced
2 tablespoons caster (superfine) sugar
3 cloves
30 g (1 oz) butter

Serves 8

Preheat oven to 180°C (350°F). Place apples into an ovenproof
dish, sprinkle with sugar and cloves. Cover and place in the oven
for about 30 minutes, or until apples are soft. Remove cloves, stir
apples until pulpy, then add butter in small pieces and leave to cool.
   Serve warm or cold with roast pork or duck.

BARBECUE SAUCE

30 g (1 oz) butter
180g (6 oz) onion, finely chopped
2 tablespoons brown sugar
1 tablespoon vinegar
1 tablespoon Worcestershire sauce
125 ml (4 fl oz) tomato sauce
60 ml (2 fl oz) water
2 tablespoons lemon juice

Serves 4–6

Melt butter in a saucepan and add onion. Sauté until golden.
Add remaining ingredients and bring to the boil, then reduce heat
and simmer for 15 minutes.
    Serve with barbecued sausages, steak and hamburgers.

GRAVY

pan juices from roast meat
2–3 tablespoons plain (all-purpose) flour
500 ml (1 pint) beef stock, or water
salt and pepper, to taste

Serves 6–8

After removing the roast from your baking tray, leave in about
250 ml (8 fl oz) of pan juices to make the gravy.
    Place the tray on the stove-top, over a medium heat, and
sprinkle flour over pan juices. Stir with a wooden spoon until
mixture thickens. Add stock, stirring constantly, and simmer gently
for 5–10 minutes. Add a little extra stock or water if necessary.
Season with salt or pepper.

BÉCHAMEL SAUCE

315 ml (10½ fl oz) milk
1 onion, quartered
1 stalk celery, chopped
1 carrot, chopped
6 black peppercorns
1 blade of mace
1 bay leaf
2 cloves
30 g (1 oz) butter
2 tablespoons plain (all-purpose) flour
salt and freshly ground black pepper, to taste

Serves 6

Place milk, onion, celery, carrot, peppercorns, mace, bay leaf
and cloves in the top of a double boiler over gently boiling water.
Cover the pan and heat very slowly for 30 minutes. Strain and set
milk aside.

   Melt butter in a heavy saucepan, stir in flour and cook
for 1 minute over a medium heat. Add milk and heat, stirring
constantly until boiling. Reduce heat to low and cook for 2 minutes.
Season with salt and pepper.

BÉARNAISE SAUCE

1 shallot (scallion), chopped
½–1 tablespoons tarragon, chopped
sprig thyme
1 bay leaf
2 tablespoons tarragon vinegar
2 egg yolks
pinch of cayenne pepper
salt and freshly ground black pepper, to taste
1–2 tablespoons lemon juice or white wine vinegar
90 g (3 oz) butter

Serves 4

In a small saucepan, infuse shallot, a little tarragon, thyme and bay
leaf in vinegar for 2 minutes. Bring this mixture to the boil, then
simmer for 2–3 minutes. Strain.

Using a double boiler (or a bowl over a saucepan), place the
egg yolks, seasonings and lemon juice into the top of the pan.
Whisk over hot water until the sauce begins to thicken. Add the
butter, in very small pieces, whisking in each piece until completely
melted before adding the next – do not allow to boil, or it will
curdle. If the sauce is too thick, add a little cream.

BOLOGNESE SAUCE

250 g (8 oz) lean steak, finely chopped
250 g (8 oz) lean pork, finely chopped
60 g (2 oz) bacon or prosciutto, chopped
1 tablespoon olive oil
4 cloves garlic, peeled and chopped
1 large onion, finely chopped
1 tablespoon parsley, chopped
1 x 500 g (16 oz) can whole tomatoes, peeled
250 ml (8 fl oz) red wine (optional)
125 ml (4 fl oz) water
2 tablespoons tomato paste
salt and freshly ground black pepper, to taste
1 bay leaf
½ bunch fresh basil, chopped

Serves 4

In a bowl, mix steak, pork and bacon together well. Heat oil in a
saucepan, then add meat, garlic, onion and parsley and fry until
meat is cooked.

Add tomatoes (with juice from can), wine, water, tomato paste,
salt and pepper and bay leaf. Cover and simmer for 1–2 hours.
Remove bay leaf and add basil 5 minutes before the end of
cooking time.

The longer the sauce is cooked, the more flavor it will have.
Check that the sauce isn't drying up while cooking. If necessary,
add more wine or water.

CAVIAR MAYONNAISE

250 ml (8 fl oz) mayonnaise (see page 367)
250 g (8 fl oz) sour cream
1 tablespoon lemon juice
2 teaspoons French mustard
30 g (1 oz) black caviar
salt and freshly ground black pepper, to taste

Serves 6

Combine all ingredients in a bowl and mix together well.

CHOCOLATE SAUCE

60 g (2 oz) chocolate, roughly chopped
150 ml (5 fl oz) boiling water
1 tablespoon cornflour (cornstarch)
2 tablespoons cold water
250 g (8 oz) caster (superfine) sugar
60 g (2 oz) butter
60 ml (2 fl oz) brandy or rum (optional)

Serves 6–8

Add chocolate to simmering water in a saucepan. Heat gently until chocolate melts and mixture is smooth. In a cup, blend cornflour to a smooth paste with cold water. Add sugar, then cornflour paste, to chocolate mixture. Bring to the boil, stirring continuously until sugar is dissolved and sauce has thickened. Simmer for 3 minutes, then stir in butter and brandy or rum (if using).

DILL SAUCE

60 g (2 oz) softened butter
1 teaspoon lemon juice
½ teaspoon dried dill
250 ml (8 fl oz) mayonnaise (see page 367)
½ teaspoon caster (superfine) sugar

Serves 10

In a bowl, blend softened butter with remaining ingredients, and beat well. Transfer mixture to a saucepan and heat gently. Do not boil. Serve with chicken or lamb.

FRENCH DRESSING

3 parts oil
1 part vinegar
salt and freshly ground black pepper, to taste

Serves 6

Crushed garlic, French or English mustard and chopped herbs can
be added. Garlic, mustard, salt and pepper are first mixed with
the oil, then vinegar is added and all are well mixed. Herbs are
added last.

GRAPEFRUIT BUTTER

500 g (1 lb) caster (superfine) sugar
125 g (4 oz) butter
250 ml (8 fl oz) grapefruit juice
2 teaspoons grapefruit rind, finely grated
5 eggs, well beaten

Makes about 1 L (2 pints)

Place sugar, butter, grapefruit juice and rind into the top of a double
boiler. Stir over simmering water until butter is melted and sugar
is dissolved.

Add eggs and keep stirring over simmering water until mixture
thickens and coats the back of a spoon (about 1 hour).

Bottle mixture in sterilized jars. Seal and label. Grapefruit butter
will keep well in the refrigerator for 2 weeks.

HONEY LEMON BUTTER

5 eggs, well beaten
125 ml (4 fl oz) honey
125 g (4 oz) butter, softened
250 g (8 oz) caster (superfine) sugar
250 ml (8 fl oz) lemon juice
2 teaspoons lemon rind, finely grated

Makes about 750 ml (1 ½ pints)

Combine all ingredients in top of double boiler. Stir over simmering water until thickened (about 1 hour).

Bottle mixture in sterilized jars. Seal and label. Honey Lemon Butter will keep well in the refrigerator for 2 weeks.

PARMESAN, GARLIC AND PARSLEY BUTTER

100 g softened butter
3 tablespoons finely grated Parmesan cheese
1 garlic clove, crushed
2 tablespoons chopped flat-leaf parsley
salt and pepper, to taste

Makes about 150 g (5 oz)

Mix the ingredients in a bowl until smooth.

Place the mixture onto a piece of plastic wrap and roll into a tube shape, twisting the ends and tie.

Place in the freezer until firm, then cut into slices just before use.

CUCUMBER SOUR CREAM SAUCE

1 green cucumber, peeled and seeds removed
1 x 300 g (9 oz) carton sour cream
1 clove garlic, crushed
1 tablespoon lemon juice
pinch of ground black pepper

Makes 375 ml (12 ½ fl oz)

Chop cucumber roughly and place in blender or food processor with half the sour cream. Cover and blend for a few seconds. Place blended mixture in a bowl and stir in remaining sour cream, garlic, lemon juice and pepper. Serve with new potatoes or as a dressing for potato salad.

Note: For a thinner consistency, blend all the sour cream with the cucumber in the beginning.

HOLLANDAISE SAUCE

2 egg yolks
pinch of cayenne pepper
salt and freshly ground black pepper, to taste
1–2 tablespoons lemon juice or white wine vinegar
90 g (3 oz) butter

Serves 4–6

Put egg yolks, seasonings and lemon juice into the top of a
double boiler, and water into the bottom. Bring water to the boil.
Whisk mixture over boiling water until sauce begins to thicken.
Add butter, in very small pieces, whisking in each piece until
completely melted before adding the next – do not allow sauce to
boil, or it will curdle. If the sauce is too thick, add a little cream.

HORSERADISH CREAM

250 ml (8 fl oz) fresh cream
salt and ground black pepper, to taste
pinch of paprika
125 ml (4 fl oz) horseradish relish
1 tablespoon chives, chopped

Serves 4–6

In a bowl, whip cream until stiff, then fold in remaining ingredients.
Chill for half an hour before serving. Serve with roast meat, steak
or potatoes.

WHITE SAUCE

30 g (1 oz) butter
30 g (1 oz) plain (all-purpose) flour
315 ml (10 ½ fl oz) milk
salt
nutmeg or freshly ground black pepper, to taste

Serves 4–6

Melt butter in a saucepan over a low heat, then remove from heat and stir in flour. Return to heat and cook gently for a few minutes, making sure that the roux does not brown. Remove pan from heat and gradually blend in cold milk. Replace pan on heat and bring to the boil. Reduce heat and cook, stirring with a wooden spoon, until smooth. Season well. If any lumps have formed, whisk briskly.

Variation: The amount of milk you use determines the consistency of the sauce. For coating consistency use 315 ml (1¼ cups) milk; for a thin sauce for soups use 625 ml (2½ cups); and for binding consistency use 150 ml (²/₃ cup).

ITALIAN TOMATO SAUCE

2 tablespoons olive oil
1 small onion, finely chopped
2 cloves garlic, crushed
1 kg (2 lb) tomatoes, skinned, seeded and chopped
    or 2 x 440 g (14 oz) can whole tomatoes, diced
½ teaspoon salt
½ teaspoon caster (superfine) sugar, or to taste
¼ teaspoon freshly ground black pepper
2 leaves basil
1 sprig oregano
1 bay leaf
1 tablespoon tomato paste

Serves 4

In a large saucepan, heat oil. Add onion and garlic and
cook for 5–6 minutes, stirring until onion is translucent.
Add tomatoes and all other ingredients. Return to heat and bring
to the boil. Reduce heat, cover, and simmer for 45 minutes,
stirring occasionally.

    Purée sauce in a blender or food processor if you want a
smooth consistency.

MAYONNAISE

1–2 egg yolks
1 teaspoon white wine vinegar
½ teaspoon salt
½ teaspoon dry mustard
pinch of white pepper
150 ml (5 fl oz) olive oil
few drops of lemon juice

Makes 250 ml (8 fl oz)

Make sure your bowl is well washed and dried. In it beat egg yolks,
vinegar, salt, dry mustard and pepper with an egg beater or an
electric beater set at medium speed.

Add olive oil, drop by drop, whisking continuously, until about
2 tablespoons have been added. Add a few drops of lemon juice,
to bring mixture to the consistency of cream. Add the remaining
oil in a thin steady stream, beating continuously, stopping the
addition of the oil from time to time to make sure the mixture is
combining well.

When all the oil has been added and the mayonnaise is thick, add
extra lemon juice to taste. Adjust seasoning. Mayonnaise will keep
for 5–7 days in a sealed container in the refrigerator.

Note: If the mixture curdles, wash the beater, beat 1 egg yolk in
another bowl and very slowly add the curdled mayonnaise to the
fresh egg yolk, beating continuously.

TARTAR SAUCE

150 ml (5 fl oz) mayonnaise (see page 367)
1 teaspoon capers, chopped
1 teaspoon gherkin, chopped
1 teaspoon parsley, freshly chopped
½ teaspoon dried tarragon
½ teaspoon dried chervil
pinch of caster (superfine) sugar
salt and freshly ground black pepper, to taste

Serves 4

Combine all ingredients and season with salt and pepper.
This sauce is delicious served with oysters, shrimp or fillets of fish.
Keeps in the refrigerator for 5–7 days.

SMOKY BARBECUE MARINADE

1 tablespoon smoked paprika
2 tablespoons brown sugar
2 garlic cloves, finely chopped
125 ml (4 fl oz) golden syrup
1 tablespoon white wine vinegar
1 tablespoon olive oil
2 tablespoon barbecue sauce

In a mixing bowl, combine paprika, brown sugar, garlic, golden
syrup, white wine vinegar, olive oil and barbecue sauce and
mix well.

MINT SAUCE

2 heaped tablespoons mint leaves
2 teaspoons caster (superfine) sugar
½ teaspoon hot water
2 tablespoons vinegar

Serves 2

Wash and dry mint leaves, then put them on a chopping board with
1 teaspoon sugar (this helps you chop the mint finely). Chop until
fine, then put into a sauceboat. Add the rest of the sugar, stir
in the hot water and leave for a few minutes, to dissolve sugar.
Add the vinegar.

PARSLEY BUTTER

60 g (2 oz) butter
1 teaspoon parsley, finely chopped
2 teaspoons lemon juice

Makes 65 g (2 oz)

In a bowl, beat the butter until light and creamy. Beat in parsley and
lemon juice. Chill well before serving.

QUICK TOMATO SAUCE

30 g (1 oz) butter
1 small onion, grated
1 small apple, grated
2 teaspoons cornflour (cornstarch)
315 ml (10 ½ fl oz) water
salt and freshly ground black pepper, to taste
1 x 150 g (5 oz) can tomato paste
good pinch of caster (superfine) sugar

Makes 500 ml (1 pint)

Heat butter in a saucepan. Fry onion for a few minutes, then the apple until soft. In a bowl, blend cornflour with water and salt and pepper. Add tomato paste and cornflour mixture to saucepan. Bring mixture to the boil and stir until smooth and thickened. Simmer gently for about 10 minutes, then taste, adjust seasonings and add sugar. Serve warm.

PEANUT SAUCE

60 g (2 oz) butter
1 onion, finely chopped
1 clove garlic, crushed
1 tablespoon soy sauce
1 tablespoon peanut butter
1 teaspoon lemon juice
125 ml (4 fl oz) fresh cream

Makes 300 ml (10 fl oz)

Heat butter in a saucepan, then sauté onion and garlic until golden.
Add soy sauce, peanut butter and lemon juice and mix thoroughly.
Remove sauce from heat and cool. Before serving, add the cream.
This sauce is delicious with barbecued steak and chops.

PLUM SAUCE

250 g (8 oz) plum jam
75 ml (2 ½ fl oz) mango chutney
75 ml (2 ½ fl oz) mango nectar
1 tablespoon vinegar
1 teaspoon caster (superfine) sugar

Makes 400 ml (13 fl oz)

In a bowl, mix plum jam with mango chutney and nectar.
Purée mixture in a blender or food processor. In a saucepan, heat
vinegar, add sugar and stir until dissolved. Add jam mixture and
beat well.

SWEET AND SOUR SAUCE

1 tablespoon cornflour (cornstarch)
1 tablespoon soy sauce
185 ml (6 fl oz) white vinegar
185 ml (6 fl oz) caster (superfine) sugar
250 ml (8 fl oz) chicken stock (see page 377)
1 green capsicum (bell pepper), seeded and sliced
250 g (8 oz) pineapple pieces
1 small carrot, thinly sliced
1 teaspoon fresh ginger, finely chopped

Serves 6–8

In a cup, blend cornflour and soy sauce together until smooth.
Place in a sauce-pan with vinegar, sugar and chicken stock.
Bring to the boil, stirring continuously. Simmer for 5 minutes.

Meanwhile, blanch capsicum and drain it. Add pineapple,
capsicum, carrot and ginger to sauce. Heat gently and
serve immediately.

VANILLA CUSTARD SAUCE

315 ml (½ pint) milk
½ teaspoon vanilla essence
3 tablespoons caster sugar
3 egg yolks

Serves 4–6

In a saucepan, heat milk over a low heat. Add vanilla essence and stir through. In a bowl, mix sugar and egg yolks until smooth. Add a little of the warmed milk to the egg mixture, stirring constantly, then add remaining milk.

Return mixture to the saucepan, still on a low heat, and stir constantly, until the mixture thickens and has the consistency of cream (it should coat the back of a metal spoon). Serve warm with ice cream, baked and steamed puddings or fruit puddings.

This sauce will keep well in the refrigerator for 3–4 days.

SALAD DRESSING

1 lemon juice
2 tablespoons Dijon mustard
250 ml (8 fl oz) olive oil
1 teaspoon salt
80 ml (2²/₃ fl oz) balsamic vinegar
1 clove garlic, crushed
1 teaspoon fresh basil, finely chopped

Makes 375 ml (1½ cups)

In a bowl, mix all ingredients well until combined.

SEAFOOD DRESSING

125 ml (4 fl oz) tomato ketchup
125 g (4 fl oz) mayonnaise (see page 367)
125 ml (4 fl oz) fresh cream

Serves 4

Mix all ingredients together and chill before serving.
    Dressing will keep well in the refrigerator for 5–7 days.

THOUSAND ISLAND DRESSING

250 ml (8 fl oz) mayonnaise (see page 367)
2 tablespoons tomato ketchup
2 tablespoons chilli sauce (optional)
2 tablespoons green olives, finely chopped
1 tablespoons chives, finely chopped
2 tablespoons whipped cream

Serves 6

In a bowl, combine all ingredients well. Chill before serving.

HONEY LEMON MUSTARD DRESSING

juice of ½ a lemon
2 tablespoons honey
3 tablespoons olive oil
2 tablespoons Dijon mustard
salt and pepper, to taste

Add all of the ingredients to a small jar and shake to combine. Note:
Store for up to 7 days in an airtight container in the fridge.

STOCK

BEEF STOCK

1 kg (2 lb) shin of beef, finely sliced
3.8 L (7 pints) cold water
60 g (2 oz) butter
1 carrot, thinly sliced
1 parsnip, thinly sliced
1 turnip, thinly sliced
1 onion, thinly sliced
2 stalks celery, thinly sliced
1 large tomato, finely chopped
salt and freshly ground black pepper, to taste

Makes 3.8 L (7 pints)

Place beef in a large saucepan. Add water, making sure it covers beef, and bring to the boil. Cover and simmer for 30 minutes. Chill. Remove surface fat, skim off floating particles and strain.

Melt butter in a large saucepan and fry vegetables over a moderate heat for 10 minutes, being careful not to let onion burn. Add strained liquid and salt and pepper, then bring liquid to the boil. Simmer, covered, for 2 hours. Strain stock. Let it cool, and keep it in the refrigerator.

Will keep up to 3 days in the refrigerator or 3 months in the freezer.

CHICKEN STOCK

1 chicken, fat removed
3.8 L (7 pints) cold water
1 carrot
1 parsnip
4 stalks celery
1 white onion
60 g (2 oz) butter
6 sprigs parsley
salt and freshly ground black pepper, to taste

Makes 3.8 L (7 pints)

Place chicken in a large saucepan. Add water, making sure
it covers chicken, and bring to the boil. Cover and simmer for
30 minutes, then chill. Remove surface fat and strain liquid.
Rinse semi-cooked carcass with warm water.

Cut vegetables into 5 mm (¼ in) slices. Melt butter in a large
saucepan and fry vegetables over moderate heat for 10 minutes.
Do not let onion burn. Add strained liquid together with chicken
and parsley. Simmer, covered, for 2 hours, skimming surface
occasionally. Add salt and pepper. Remove chicken and strain
stock. Cool stock and store in the refrigerator.

FISH STOCK

750 g (1½ lb) fish bones and trimmings
1 tomato, chopped
2 sprigs parsley
1 bay leaf
1 large onion, sliced
1 clove garlic, crushed
2 teaspoons salt
6 black peppercorns
2.2 L (5 pints) cold water

Makes 2.2 L (4 pints)

Wash fish bones or trimmings well. Place in a large saucepan with other ingredients. Cover saucepan and bring to the boil. Reduce heat and simmer for 1 hour. Strain before using.

WEIGHTS & MEASUREMENTS

Temperature
100°C = 200°F
120°C = 250°F
140°C = 280°F
150°C = 300°F
165°C = 325°F
180°C = 350°F
190°C = 375°F
200°C = 400°F
220°C = 420°F
250°C = 485°F

Fluid measures
60 ml = 2 fl oz
90 ml = 3 fl oz
125 ml = 4 fl oz
250 ml = 8 fl oz
570 ml = 1 pint
1 L = 1.8 pints

Solid measures
10 g = $\frac{1}{3}$ oz
20 g = $\frac{2}{3}$ oz
30 g = 1 oz
40 g = 1½ oz
60 g = 2 oz
80 g = 2½ oz
100 g = 3½ oz
120 g = 4 oz
150 g = 5 oz
160 g = 5½ oz
180 g = 6 oz
200 g = 7 oz
250 g = 8 oz
300 g = 10 oz
350 g = 11½ oz
400 g = 14 oz
500 g = 1 lb
750 g = 1½ lb
1 kg = 2 lb

INDEX